Justin McCarthy

The Epoch of Reform

Justin McCarthy

The Epoch of Reform

ISBN/EAN: 9783337297176

Printed in Europe, USA, Canada, Australia, Japan

Cover: Foto ©ninafisch / pixelio.de

More available books at **www.hansebooks.com**

Epochs of Modern History

THE

EPOCH OF REFORM

1830–1850

BY

JUSTIN McCARTHY, M. P.

AUTHOR OF "A HISTORY OF OUR OWN TIMES"

NEW YORK
CHARLES SCRIBNER'S SONS

PREFACE.

———•———

THE object of this little book is, in the first instance, to give a clear and concise account of the changes in our political system, from the introduction of Lord Grey's first Reform Bill to the death of Sir Robert Peel. That epoch of Reform encloses a group of constitutional changes so important as to entitle it to a distinct place in the history of England. Lord Grey's Reform Bill established the basis of a popular suffrage, gave representation to the great industrial towns, and abolished many old standing anomalies and sources of corruption. The tithe system was brought to an end in Ireland. Slavery was banished from our colonies for ever. The working of women and children in mines and factories was placed under wholesome regulation. The foundation of a system of national education was laid. Our penal code was made human and reasonable. The corn laws were repealed. These changes, and others hardly less important, are the birth of that marvellous period of political activity. Moreover, during this epoch of Reform the relations of the Sovereign to Parliament,

and of Parliament to the People, were established on a
well defined and satisfactory principle.

The manner in which all these changes were
brought about is a lesson of the deepest political
interest to every student. I have been especially
anxious to show how the policy which opens the way
to Reform is the true antidote to the spirit of Revolution. Some of the grievances under which the
English people suffered before this epoch of Reform
were severe enough to have warranted an attempt at
Revolution, if no other means of relief seemed attain-
able, and if that desperate remedy had some chance
of success. Revolution, however, was avoided in
England because English statesmen had learnt the
wisdom which statesmen on the Continent had not
acquired—the wisdom which teaches a Minister when
to make his own opinions and prejudices give way
before the pressure of evidence and experience, and
of opinions that have not yet become his own. That
was the wisdom which English Ministers during that
epoch proved themselves especially to possess. They
were not for the most part men of great intellect or
political genius. Some of the continental statesmen
whose mistakes and perversity brought misfortune on
their country were men of higher intellectual grasp than
some of the English Ministers whose shrewd sound
judgment saved England from the peril of Revolution.
But the manner in which England was governed during

the period I have described, made it evident to all that every change in our political 'system needed for the good of the nation can be obtained by the patient and persistent use of argument and of reason, without any thought of an ultimate appeal to force. This, in itself, is the true principle of political freedom.

I have endeavoured to give my readers something like a picture of each leading public man on both sides of politics during this epoch of Reform. The more vividly we can form an impression as to the appearance, the bearing, and the personal peculiarities of a statesman, the more likely are we to understand the part he took in public affairs, and the purposes and principles which inspired him. The National Portrait Gallery in London is a valuable instructor even to the profoundest student of English history. No period of equal length in that history encloses a greater number of remarkable figures than the statesmen, orators, and politicians from Lord Grey, Lord John Russell, and O'Connell, to Sir Robert Peel, Lord Palmerston, and Mr. Cobden.

CHRONOLOGICAL TABLE OF CONTENTS.

———◆———

Contents.

PRIME MINISTERS. 1830—1850.

Duke of Wellington . . . . . Jan. 25, 1828 to Nov. 22, 1830.
Earl Grey . . . . Nov. 22, 1830 " July 18, 1834.
Lord Melbourne . . . . July 18, 1834 " Dec. 26, 1834.
Sir Robert Peel . . . . Dec. 26, 1834 " April 18, 1835.
Lord Melbourne . . . . April 18, 1835 " Sept. 6, 1841.
Sir Robert Peel . . . . Sept. 6, 1841 " July 6, 1846.
Lord John Russell . . . . . . July 6, 1846 " Feb. 24, 1851.

ADMINISTRATIONS. 1830—1850.

1. 1828. DUKE OF WELLINGTON'S MINISTRY.

Prime Minister . . . . Duke of Wellington.
Lord Chancellor . . . . Lord Lyndhurst.
Chancellor of Exchequer . . . Mr. H. Goulburn.
Home Secretary . . . . Sir R. Peel.
Foreign   "   . . . . Lord Aberdeen.
Colonial   "   . . . . Sir George Murray.
Secretary at War . . . . Sir Henry Hardinge.
First Lord of the Admiralty . . Lord Melville, succeded by Sir
James Graham.

2. 1830. THE REFORM MINISTRY.

Prime Minister . . . . Earl Grey.
Lord Chancellor . . . . Lord Brougham.
Chancellor of Exchequer . . . Lord Althorp.
Home Secretary . . . . Lord Melbourne.

Foreign Secretary . . . . . . Lord Palmerston.

Colonial Secretary . . . . . . Lord Goderich, afterwards Mr. Stanley.

Secretary at War . . . . Mr. C. N. W. Wynn, not in the Cabinet.

First Lord of the Admiralty . . Sir. J. R. Graham.

Lord John Russell was Paymaster of the Forces but not in the Cabinet.

Mr. Stanley and Sir James Graham resigned office in 1834 upon the Irish Church question, and were succeeded by Mr. Spring Rice and Lord Auckland.

In July, 1834, Earl Grey retired and Lord Melbourne succeeded him : the rest of the Ministers remained in office : Lord Duncannon became Home Secretary in place of Lord Melbourne.

4. 1834. SIR R. PEEL'S FIRST MINISTRY.

Prime Minister . . . . Sir R. Peel.

Lord Chancellor. . . . . Lord Lyndhurst.

Chancellor of Exchequer . . . Sir R. Peel.

Home Secretary . . . . Mr. H. Goulburn.

Foreign   "   . . . . Duke of Wellington.

Colonial   "   . . . . Earl of Aberdeen.

Secretary at War . . . . Lord Wharncliffe.

In this Ministry Mr. W. E. Gladstone was Under-Secretary for the Colonies.

5. 1834. LORD MELBOURNE'S SECOND MINISTRY.

Prime Minister . . . . Lord Melbourne.

Lord Chancellor . . . . In commission, afterwards Lord Cottenham.

Chancellor of Exchequer . . . Mr. Spring Rice.

Home Secretary . . . . Lord John Russell.

Foreign   "   . . . . Lord Palmerston.

Colonial   "   . . . . Mr. Grant.

Secretary at War . . . . Lord Howick.

First Lord of the Admiralty . . Lord Auckland.

Later Lord J. Russell became Colonial Secretary, Mr. Spring Rice entered the Upper House as Lord Monteagle, and was succeeded as Chancellor of the Exchequer by Mr. Baring: Lord Howick was succeeded at the War Office by Mr. Macaulay.

6. 1841. SIR R. PEEL'S SECOND MINISTRY.

Prime Minister . . . . Sir R. Peel.
Lord Chancellor . . . . Lord Lyndhurst.
Chancellor of Exchequer . . . Mr. Goulburn.
Home Secretary . . . . Sir James Graham.
Foreign   "   . . . . Lord Aberdeen.
Colonial   "   . . . . Lord Stanley.
Secretary of War . . . . Sir Henry Hardinge.
First Lord of the Admiralty . . Lord Haddington.
President of the Board of
    Trade . . . . Earl Ripon, afterwards Mr. Gladstone.
Without office but in the
    Cabinet . . . . Duke of Wellington.

7. 1846. LORD J. RUSSELL'S FIRST MINISTRY.

Prime Minister . . . . Lord J. Rnssell.
Lord Chancellor . . . . Lord Cottenham.
Chancellor of Exchequer . . . Mr. C. Wood.
Home Secretary . . . . Sir G. Grey.
Foreign   "   . . . . Lord Palmerston.
Colonial   "   . . . . Earl Grey (Lord Howick).
First Lord of the Admiralty . . Lord Auckland.
Paymaster General . . . . . . Mr. Macaulay.
President of the Board of
    Trade . . . . Earl of Clarendon.

THE EPOCH OF REFORM.

1830-1850.

CHAPTER I.

REFORM AND REVOLUTION.

THE epoch of Reform in England is the period of transition during which the representative system in Parliament and the constitutional system in Monarchy became settled institutions. The representative principle in Parliamentary Government is that which secures to the people the right of freely choosing an adequate number of men to speak for them in the House of Commons. The constitutional principle in Monarchy is that which requires the sovereign to act on the advice of his ministers, who are themselves responsible to Parliament, and not to attempt to govern the country according to his own notions and his own will. The epoch of Reform in England coincides very nearly with the epoch of revolution on the Continent of Europe. Where such reforms as those which took place in England are resisted by the force of arbitrary government, the natural result is revolution. As the intelligence of a people develops, and education spreads, there grows up among them a conviction that "the common sense of all," as Mr. Tennyson describes it, is better able to take care of the common interest than the arbitrary judgment of any sovereign or

B

statesman, however sagacious and well-meaning. A time comes when that conviction has taken full and firm hold of the great majority of a people, and when that time comes, it is no longer possible to prevent the accomplishment of a change in the political system. It is not possible to resist that change, any more than it is to resist the action of any physical law governing the movements of the world. No matter how strong the despotic power which endeavours to resist, the resistance is overcome in the end. The movement of civilised men is everywhere towards representative institutions, and where there is a monarchy, towards the constitutional principle in the monarchy. The wisdom of statesmen and of rulers consists in seeing when the stages of political development have been reached at which successive conditions of arbitrary rule have to give way before the popular movement. When statesmen are wise enough to see this for themselves by the light of their own intelligence, or are made to feel it by the pressure brought to bear on them and are willing to give way before the pressure, we have reform. Where this is not done we have revolt or revolution. If revolt, it is probable that after a severe strain there follows a period of reaction. But that reaction is sure to be succeeded by another period of revolt, and if the resistance of the ruling power be prolonged, there comes at last the period of revolution.

This chapter of history begins with the year 1830, after the repeal of the Test and Corporation Act, in 1828, and after the passing of the great Act of Catholic Emancipation in 1829. Such measures, great as were their results and obvious as were their justice, do not come within the sphere of that kind of political reform which is to be studied in this volume. The principle on which the admission of Dissenters to civil and municipal office, and the political emancipation of Catholics, was founded, was one of moral justice. No matter what the system of government which prevailed in England, the justice of religious equality in civil and political affairs would have been recognised in time. In some of the most despotic countries in the world there never was any idea of maintaining such a principle of religious exclusion and intolerance as that illustrated by the disenfranchisement of Roman Catholics, and the Test and Corporation Acts. Curiously enough, some of the countries which even in the present day maintain the most antique and anomalous systems of arbitrary government, have never had religious exclusiveness or religious tests as any part of their governing principle. Therefore, it is not right to regard Catholic Emancipation, the recognition of the civil rights of Dissenters, or the admission of the Jews to the House of Commons, as mere measures of political reform. The disqualification was in itself an obvious and gross outrage on the common principle of justice which must be supposed to be the basis of every state system. But while it is perfectly obvious to the modern mind that no man ought to be excluded from citizenship and its full privileges because of his religious faith, it is not by any means equally obvious that a certain proportion of persons living in houses of a certain rental should be either admitted to or excluded from the right to vote. When we come to consider that question we come into the region of pure political reform. In the same way the functions of the sovereign cannot be defined on any principle of obvious and fundamental justice. It must be a matter of growth and development, of adaptation to the wants and the condition of each particular stage of each country's growth : a matter of compromise and arrangement.

Here then, also, we have the working of the principle of political reform, The two most significant reforms accomplished and established in England during the period which this history describes are the reforms in representation and the changes gradually made in the relation of the sovereign towards the people. These principles were formally established in England between the years 1830 and 1850. No matter what further changes may take place in the governing system of this country; no matter how the functions of the sovereign may hereafter be either extended or restricted; no matter how the principle of election may be expanded or varied; all such changes can be but further developments of the principles recognised and established between 1830 and 1850. All over Europe we see the varying process of development of the same principles. In every country of the European Continent the recognition of this principle has been preceded by a period of revolution or of revolt, followed by reaction, and then revolt again. Only in England have the reforms been accomplished without a struggle. Nor is this owing, as is generally supposed, to the fact that the English political system embodied no serious grievance and no genuine oppression. On the contrary, there were many anomalies of English political life which bore down on certain classes more severely and more unjustly than such classes were borne down upon in almost any continental state. The reason why the changes in England were so quiet and so satisfactory, was that English statesmen had arrived at that condition of political intelligence which made them able to recognise the fact that changes which they themselves disliked, and would, if they could, have resisted, had nevertheless become inevitable, and must take place sooner or later, peacefully or with violence. English statesmen were fortunately able to see the immense advantage of accepting the inevitable at the right moment. Wellington and Peel saw that they could not successfully resist the changes which the Metternichs and the Polignacs believed they could successfully resist. To this fact is due the whole difference between the manner in which political changes were wrought out in this country and on the Continent. Had English statesmen been like those of foreign countries, we, too, should have had to describe the period between 1830 and 1850 as a period, not of reform, but of revolution.

In 1830 Europe was just beginning to rise from a long period of depression and of political reaction. The French Revolution had swept over the Continent as a forest fire in America flames from tree to tree. The victories of the great Napoleon set the flag of France floating in every continental capital. From the heights of Boulogne Napoleon threatened England herself with invasion. Suddenly, however, there came a turn in the tide. Napoleon attempted impossibilities, and thus brought ruin upon his ambition and himself. It has been well observed by a French writer that the great difference between Napoleon and Julius Cæsar is that Cæsar knew what he could not do as well as what he could do, and was therefore successful to the end; Napoleon did not know what he could not do, and therefore failed. Napoleon dreamed of the complete subjugation of Europe; of himself as the sole autocrat of the Continent; even of England beaten to her knees and brought under his dominion. He was not a man of sound political education, and did not thoroughly understand any country but his own. He was under the impression that the murmurs of political discontent which reached him from England really showed that the English people would be glad of a revolution effected in their country by means of an invasion from France. He had crushed Austria, Prussia, Spain, Italy, Holland, and all the continental states except Russia, and he had defeated Russia in the battle-field and forced the Czar to come to terms dictated by himself. He had set up his brothers as kings in Spain, Holland, and Westphalia; he had made his brilliant cavalry officer Murat king of Naples, and one of his marshals, Bernadotte, king of Sweden. At one point of his career Napoleon had no acknowledged enemy in Europe but England alone. Pitt, the Prime Minister, son of the great Chatham, had striven long and hard to keep up an alliance of the other European powers against Napoleon, but it had utterly failed; and Pitt never recovered from the shock given to him by the news of the crushing defeat inflicted upon Austria in the battle of Austerlitz. England stood alone against Napoleon for a long time. She was always victorious on the seas. The genius of Nelson and his successive victories kept alive the spirit and enthusiasm of the English people, even in the hours of deepest depression. At last Napoleon went so far as to issue decrees from Berlin and from Milan in which he prohibited all the European nations from trading with England. He entertained the preposterous idea that he could thus actually destroy the whole trade of England, and reduce her to something like starvation. He quarrelled anew with Russia, and entered upon the desperate scheme of an invasion of that country. Despite the fierce and patient resistance of the Russians he forced his way to Moscow. The people set their city on fire rather than endure its occupation by the French. Napoleon had to begin a retreat amid the terrible rigours of a Russian winter. The Russians harassed his retreating army at every step. The retreat was only a long series of battles. Between Russian arms and the Russian climate Napoleon lost six-sevenths of his army. He had entered Russia with more than 600,000 soldiers; he brought less than 80,000 back.

Meanwhile the Duke of Wellington had been defeating some of Napoleon's best marshals in Spain, and rendering the French occupation of that country an impossible task. Austria and Prussia had been recovering their courage and strength. The folly of Napoleon's idea, that he could really extinguish the nationality of the Germans and reduce them to the condition of abject bondmen to the power of France, soon began to show itself. Germany rose against him, and he received an overwhelming defeat at Leipzig. An alliance was again formed for the purpose of crushing him; England was the inspiring influence of the alliance; Russia, Austria, Prussia, Sweden, and other powers were joined in it. Napoleon was defeated; the allied powers entered Paris; he was deposed and sent to Elba, an islet in the Mediterranean. The allied powers left him the title of Emperor and gave him a little army with which to amuse himself. Lord John Russell visited Napoleon in Elba, and had some conversation with him. Napoleon showed how little he understood of England by telling Lord John Russell that he had no doubt the Duke of Wellington would make use of the great influence of his military success to have himself declared king of England.

The sovereigns of Europe called together a congress at Vienna for the purpose of restoring what they considered to be order, and reorganising the systems and countries which had been swept over by Napoleon's victories. The Bourbon king Louis XVIII. was set up in France. Suddenly, while the congress was sitting, Napoleon escaped from Elba, landed in France, and was welcomed everywhere by the army and the people. The congress broke up; King Louis XVIII. fled in very unkingly fashion out of the country; Napoleon was Emperor of the French once more. The allies.prepared to attack him, and pledged themselves never to rest until they had completely broken his power. The only forces immediately available were the English and the Prussians under Wellington and Blucher in Belgium. Napoleon flung himself on the Prussians and defeated them. One of the best of his splendid marshals, Ney, attacked the English at the same time, but had to fall back without success. The object of the English and the Prussians was to draw their forces together; Napoleon's purpose was to crush the English before the Prussians could come up.

Wellington took up a fine position at Waterloo, not very far from Brussels, the capital of Belgium. He was attacked by Napoleon there : he had to bear the whole brunt of the day alone, for the Prussians only came up late in the evening, and his army was not only outnumbered by that of Napoleon, but had only a comparatively small number of English, Irish, and Scotchmen in it, being in great measure made up of Belgians, Hanoverians, and Hessians. Wellington's generalship and the indomitable courage of his own men triumphed over every difficulty. The finest of the French cavalry could make no impression on them. Marshal Ney himself led more than one desperate charge. It is worth observing, to show how different the real business of a commander often is from the part which he would be made to play on the stage or in a picture, that Ney prepared for one charge by putting his sword into its sheath in order that it might be out of his way, and that Murat, the most brilliant cavalry officer of his day, hardly ever went into action with any weapon more formidable than a riding-whip in his hand. At last the Prussians came up, and the defeat of the French was complete. Napoleon had to fly for his life. He reached Paris almost alone. He abdicated the throne, went on board an English man-of-war, the Bellerophon, and surrendered himself prisoner. He was sent to exile in St. Helena, an island in the South Atlantic. Thackeray, the great novelist, when a child returning from India, was taken at St. Helena to see the fallen Emperor walking up and down his little garden. Napoleon never succeeded in regaining his freedom, and he died in St. Helena ; still, after all that wild and wonderful career, having scarcely passed middle age.

Meanwhile the Congress of Vienna set to work to restore the old conditions of things in Europe. The continental sovereigns and statesmen had not the faintest comprehension of the realities of the situation. They did not understand that Napoleon had really effaced feudalism and what was called the divine right of kings. The French Revolution, of which he had been the great weapon and instrument, had destroyed all in the old systems that really deserved destruction and had long been waiting for it. No congress, no Holy Alliance, as the union of some of the continental sovereigns was afterwards called, could restore what the Revolution had actually removed. But the continental sovereigns and statesmen did not see this, and were fully convinced that it only needed a little exertion of energy to bring back the old order of things. The Holy Alliance was framed by a convention signed with the names of Francis, Emperor of Austria, Frederick William, King of Prussia, and Alexander, Emperor of Russia. The convention declared that these sovereigns had no other object in framing the agreement than to publish to the world their

fixed resolution to take, in the administration of their own
states and in their relations with other powers, the pre-
cepts of religion for their sole guide. They therefore
pledged themselves to "remain united by the bonds of a
true and indissoluble fraternity," and to help each other
and to use their arms to protect religion, peace, and justice. Finally, the document declared that all powers
which should choose " solemnly to avow the sacred principles which have dictated the present act will be received
with equal ardour and affection into this holy alliance."
These last words gave to the alliance the name by which
it has ever since been known. It soon appeared, however, that by maintaining peace, religion, and justice, the
allied powers only meant the carrying out of their own
despotic will, and securing their own supposed interests.
They proclaimed themselves the champions and ministers of religion and justice, but reserved to themselves the
right of defining what justice and religion were. Justice
and religion meant, according to their definition, the divine right of kings, the sacredness of despotic power,
and the suppression of free speech and public liberty of
every kind, wherever they could exercise any power of
intervention.

So they complacently set to work to put back the hand
of time to the historical hour at which it was pointing
when the mob of Paris destroyed the Bastile. They restored the dethroned princes and princelings ; they sustained arbitrary authority everywhere ; they proclaimed
once again the principle of the divine right of kings ;
they put a stop to liberty of speech or publication ;
they governed by soldiers and police. They bound
themselves by the engagement from which was taken the
name of " holy alliance " to unite in putting down revolutionary agitation wherever it should show itself. For a

time, England, under such ministers as Lord Liverpool
and Lord Castlereagh, lent herself to this policy of reaction and repression. It was only when Canning, the
great parliamentary orator and statesman, came to be
really powerful that this country distinctly and finally
withdrew from any participation in the principles and the
policy of the holy alliance. Gradually the very stringency of the reaction brought about the undoing of much
of its own work. The resolve of the Bourbon Government of France to intervene in the affairs of Spain, in
order to put down popular movements there, impelled
Canning to recognise the independence of the Spanish
colonies in Mexico and South America that were then in
revolt against Spanish dominion, and thus, as he said
himself in the House of Commons, to call in the New
World to redress the balance of the Old. The allies had
joined Holland and Belgium under the crown of an
Orange Prince—a union impossible of realisation since
the days of William the Silent himself; and the result
thus far was but a growing evidence of an incompatibil-
ity which could only end, as it actually did end soon
after, in convulsion and in the total separation of the
countries thus forced together against their inclination.
The independence of Greece is due to the foreign policy
of England. Greece had long been suffering the most
cruel oppression under the rule of the Turk. A rebellion broke out among the Greeks. The English statesmen endeavoured at first to restore peace by securing
a genuine reform in the system by which Greece was
governed; but as it became more and more evident that
the Turks would not reform and that Greece would not
submit, the sympathy of England was cordially given to
the Greeks in their gallant struggle, and at last an alliance was formed by England, France, and Russia, in

which England took the lead, and the result was the establishment of Greek independence. No English statesman would accept the responsibility of the battle of Navarino, in which the Turkish fleet was destroyed by the united fleets of the allies under an English Admiral. But the policy of England had none the less brought about the freedom of Greece. In fact, the principle on which the Holy Alliance had acted tended only to accomplish the very results which it was formed to prevent. The extravagances of the French Revolution and the reckless aggressive ambition of Napoleon had set in motion that reaction which reached its height in the Holy Alliance. The Holy Alliance in its turn, by trying to suppress every free movement, made revolution unavoidable on the Continent, and opened the way for reform in England.

CHAPTER II.

ENGLAND AFTER THE WAR WITH NAPOLEON.

THE years between 1815 and 1830 were specially favourable for the growth of a spirit encouraging a new movement towards political reform. England was weary of a war which had lasted with little intermission for more than twenty-one years. Her people had had their fill of military glory, and had paid their ample share of personal and public sacrifice. Domestic improvement had long been neglected. All schemes of political reform had been thrown into the shade for the time. England and her statesmen were filled with the one paramount idea— that of crushing the national enemy. Even while the process of crushing the national enemy was going on there were a good many persons here and there who never felt quite certain whether a different kind of policy on the part of the English government might not have changed the enemy into a friend. There were many who doubted whether a different course pursued towards the French Republic might not have avoided all the hatred and all the warlike rivalry which imposed so much sacrifice on both peoples. At this distance of time we only hear of the uprising of the national spirit against Napoleon and the French, and the hatred felt for "the Corsican ogre," and the exultation of Europe over his fall. But anyone who takes the trouble to look a little closely into the history of that time will find that the sympathy which welcomed the birth of the French Republic outlived amongst certain classes in this country the errors and excesses of that Republic, and went with Napoleon long after he had ceased to represent the Republican principle. At all events, there were many who much doubted whether the triumphs which the long struggle brought to England were worth the cost and the suffering by which they were bought.

After the war was over and the nation had settled down to peace again, there came naturally a certain time of political prostration, owing in part to the reaction against the first enthusiasm created by the French Republic and the disappointment of so many generous hopes, which, like those of Fox, were founded on the uprising of that great new principle in Europe. But the continuance of peace brought a revival of domestic prosperity, and with it a revival of the feelings which make for political reform. Mr. Walpole in his " History of England " justly observes, in contrasting the England of 1830 with the England of 1815, that in 1815 legislation had been directed to secure the advantage of a class. During the interval between 1815 and 1830 most of the sinecures established for the benefit of the higher classes had been abolished. It seems now almost incomprehensible that people should have endured so long the existence of many of those gross and monstrous sinecures—offices with large pay and no duties—invented for the purpose of pensioning some bankrupt member of the aristocracy. The practice which allowed public officers to discharge their duties by deputies had also been to a great extent abolished. Roman Catholics were allowed to sit in Parliament. Dissenters might hold all manner of civil and political offices. A Jew might be a civic officer of London. In commercial legislation the principle of reform was making its appearance also. In foreign policy there was a reaction going on against the principles of the Holy Alliance and "the crowned conspirators of Verona," as Sydney Smith called them, and there was a tendency to recognise that principle of nationalities which has inspired so profoundly the foreign policy of our own time. The criminal code had been mitigated by the abolition of some of its most cruel excesses. The Chancery Courts and Ecclesiastical Courts had felt the influence of the growing spirit of inquiry and of reformation.

It would not have been possible that political reform should remain long inactive under conditions so favourable to the development of reasonable principles in every other direction. At the same time that all this improvement was making itself manifest, the condition of the labouring classes in the counties was not growing better. Perhaps it would be rash to say that the labouring poor were positively worse off in 1830 than they had been half a century before, but at least they were relatively worse off. Their condition had not improved in any sense, while the artisans in the towns were getting more pros-

perous and more intelligent and more capable of acting
in combination. The manufacturing power of England
had grown immensely. New inventions, new appliances
in almost every department of industrial science were
giving fresh employment in every direction. Even the
very mechanism which the artisans dreaded and detested
at first, under the idea that it would interfere with man's
labour and his wages, was obviously operating only to
increase the amount of employment in all the manufacturing centres of the country. Here we have three conditions each acting in its own way as an influence in
favour of political reform. War is over and there seems
no prospect of its return ; artisans in towns are better
paid and more self-reliant than they were ; labourers in
the counties are, if not poorer, certainly no better off
than at any previous time. The interval of peace gives
men leisure to think of domestic politics. The sinking,
or apparently sinking, condition of the labouring classes
in the counties, where privilege is strongest, shows the
necessity for some step of reform being undertaken ; and
the working classes in the cities better paid, more independent and more capable of combination than ever they
had been before, furnish a kind of reserve force at the
command of political reformers.

Many causes had operated to throw the artisan
classes of the northern and midland towns into hostility
against Tory principles and Governments. The memory
of the Blanketeers was still fresh in the public mind. In
1817 some starving colliers of the North had thought of
making a pilgrimage to the house of the Prince Regent in
London, in the hope of being allowed to tell their tale of
misery to him, and induce him to do something on their
behalf. Following the example of those poor fellows, a
large body of Manchester working men resolved that

they would walk to London, make known their grievances to the authorities there, and ask for parlimentary
reform as one means of improving their condition. The
plan was that each pilgrim was to carry a blanket with
him, so that they might rest by the way at any chance
place of shelter. For this they were called Blanketeers.
The Government regarded this harmless movement in
exactly the same light as the Government of Louis the
Sixteenth's earliest years had regarded the attempt of a
starving crowd to excite the compassion of the sovereign :
" And so, on May 2, 1775, these vast multitudes do here
at Versailles château, in widespread wretchedness, in
sallow faces, squalor, winged raggedness, present, as in
legible hieroglyphic writing, their Petition of Grievances.
The château gates must be shut ; but the king will appear on the balcony and speak to them. They have
seen the king's face ; their Petition of Grievances has
been, if not read, looked at. For answer two of them are
hanged on a ' new gallows forty feet high,' and the rest
driven back to their dens for a time." No leader of
the Blanketeers was hanged, but some of them were
seized and imprisoned. Troops were placed along the
line of march ; many of the pilgrims were sent back to
their dens again ; others were thrown into prison forth-
with.

It is needless to say that these high-handed measures
did not prevail on people to be content with their condition, to refrain from holding meetings, and renounce their
demand for political reform. A very widespread and
vehement agitation sprang up. Manchester took a leading part in it. Most of the towns in the North fermented
with it. Orator Hunt, as he was called, a Radical
agitator and stump speaker, became famous for a moment
as a hopeful leader. He found his level afterwards

in the House of Commons, and the recognition of
the principle of reform would in any case probably have
extinguished him, for he was not in any sense a genuine
orator or even a great demagogue. But the Government
set about to deal with the agitation in a fashion which
made agitation popular and widespread, and the same
sort of policy made Orator Hunt into a popular idol,
and brought the condition of England, to adopt Mr.
Gladstone's famous phrase, " within a measurable distance
of civil war. " On August 16, 1819, a great meeting was
held in the large field near St. Peter's Church, Manchester, the spot on which the Free Trade Hall now stands.
About 80,000 persons seem to have been present, and
Orator Hunt was to be the hero of the day. Special Constables and Yeomanry were present in large numbers.
When Hunt began to speak some movement took place
amongst the Yeomanry which the crowd interpreted as
an attempt to disperse them. The Yeomanry seem themselves to have been alarmed by the swaying motions of
the crowd. The result was an unlucky demonstration of
authority on the one side, and a counter demonstration of force on the other. The Riot Act was read. Hunt
was arrested the moment he began to speak. He gave
himself up quietly, recommended peace and order to the
crowd, and was taken to the prison—for no offence that
anyone could see. A scene of confusion took place
which has never been clearly explained, but at last the
Yeomanry rode at the crowd flourishing their swords.
The immense size and weight of the crowd rendered its
dispersion impossible, and the result was that many poor
people were trampled under the feet of the horses or
sabred by the swords of the Yeomanry. Some of the
crowd flung stones at the horsemen. Altogether between
three and four hundred persons were more or less injured.

C

Every attempt to have the action of the Yeomanry pun-
ished or even rebuked proved hopeless. The event was
long afterwards remembered as the massacre of Peterloo.
Its immediate effect was to swell up the fire of anger on
both sides into something that seemed to threaten a dangerous explosion.

The Government had no idea of dealing with the crisis
in any other way than by bringing in new measures
authorising them to search for arms and seize them, to
disperse great popular meetings, to punish seditious publications, and to apply the principle of coercion everywhere. Any coercion Bill was sure to be carried by a
large majority of the House of Commons, but any proposal to inquire into the causes of the existing discontents
and distress had little chance of obtaining even a decent
number of supporters.

The one great reform which, articulately or inarticulate-
ly, the public voice began now to demand, was a measure
which should make the House of Commons a representative institution.   This was a change to be accomplished
by law.   There was, however, another reform necessary
to be effected in order to make the English Government
constitutional in the true sense. This latter reform did
not require legislative action to give it effect, and, indeed,
could hardly be brought about by any Act of Parliament.
It was a change in the relations of the Sovereign to the
Ministry and to the House of Commons, a change which
should make the majority of the House of Commons
practically supreme over the Sovereign as well as over
the Ministry. The one reform, as we shall presently see,
brought about the other.

The representation of the people of these countries was
in an anomalous condition. The House of Commons
did not, in any sense, fairly represent the nation. The

theory of a representative constitution is very simple. It is founded on what may be called an ordinary principle of business. There is no mystery about it, and no profound philosophy. It is simply the principle that every man understands best his own business, and that for a Government to get to understand the best way to manage the affairs of a country the surest method is to get as nearly as possible the opinion of every man in the country. Out of all these opinions a reasonable Government is supposed to be able to form a general idea of what the wishes of the country are, and it is fairly to be supposed that the common wish of the country will in ordinary cases tend in the direction of the country's welfare. Now, as it is not possible that each man shall give his opinion and have his say in public affairs, the principle of representation forces itself into recognition. Certain spokesmen are chosen by the people, or at least by those of the people who are electors and have the votes, and the spokesmen represent the views of those who have chosen them. Thus in a constitutional assembly the Government will always have the advantage of hearing the opinions of the majority in each constituency and also of the minority throughout the whole country. In truth this principle of representation really belongs in more or less crude form to every system of government. There used to be at one time a great deal of speculation as to the relative advantages of a representative system and of what was called a benevolent despotism. But, in fact, the comparison is one that cannot be fairly made. There is no absolute despotism in countries which have emerged even from the rudest forms of barbarism. No one man really exercises an unlimited and unconditional sway over a people, and manages their affairs " out of his own head," or according to his own caprice. In every state, however despotic its constitution may seem to be, the Sovereign has to take into account the feelings and opinions of those over whom he rules. Whether he does this perfectly or imperfectly, whether by means of a recognised representative system or by means of inquiries and investigation made through his agents and his creatures, the principle is the same. He has to consult and does consult what he believes to be the general wish of his people. The Sultan Haroun Alraschid goes forth at night in disguise and wanders through the streets of Bagdad to find out what the people are saying. Louis the Great endeavours to get at what people are saying through the medium of police spies and court gossip. Napoleon I. sets himself to work to manufacture a public opinion which may supply the place of the genuine article, and may support him in every enterprise which he feels inclined to undertake. The Emperor Nicholas of Russia condescends to confer with his council of notables, and endeavours to get at the opinions of the various governments and provinces of his Empire. No ruler, however autocratic, ventures to govern in absolute independence of the opinions of his subjects. He gets some hint at public opinion through police reports, through epigrams; or at last through infernal machines, Orsini bombs, daggers, dynamite. What men think will be made known.

Where a constitutional principle is recognised, and where the system of open representation is admitted, it is obviously of the utmost importance that the system shall be genuine, and shall answer the purposes it professes to attain. The benevolent despot, making his inquiries after his own fashion, would be much more likely to get a just notion of what his people wanted than the so-called constitutional Sovereign who relied upon an inadequate and imperfect system of representation. There never was a time in England when the authority of the Sovereign was held to be absolute over the people, and when the King, in his dealings with any class or person of the community, was supposed to have the same kind of power which some of the peasantry of Russia are still willing to believe is possessed by their Czar. For generations in England the only absolute authority claimed for or by the Sovereign, was an authority over his Ministers ; these were, in fact, considered his Ministers in the strictest sense, his subordinates, his clerks, the officers of his authority, the instruments of his will. Down almost to 1830, it was still the habit of the Sovereign to govern the country, when he chose, with a set of Ministers who were continually outvoted and censured in the House of Commons. The king, up to the same period, did really exercise the right which now exists only as a name, that of appointing and dismissing Ministers to suit his own will and pleasure. The great change which in our time has been brought about makes it certain that although there be no written law or constitutional precept to enforce it, the Sovereign no longer chooses or dismisses Ministers, except with reference to the expressed will of the nation through its representative chamber. It is impossible in our time to suppose that a Sovereign could attempt to return to the principles so completely, although so silently, abolished. A country is a constitutional country only when this change has been accomplished. The transition which was made by England in the period between the reign of George III. and the first few years of the reign of Queen Victoria, was, in this respect, as important a reform as any which could be effected in our Parliamentary institutions.

Although this little history does not deal with the story

of Catholic emancipation, it is of material bearing on our task to point out the result of the manner in which Catholic emancipation was granted. The world has justly praised the wisdom of English statesmen like Wellington and Peel, who would have refused Catholic emancipation if they could, but yet saw that the time had come when they could no longer safely refuse it. Undoubtedly, by the adoption of such a political principle English statesmen have more than once avoided revolution. But while avoiding a greater they established a lesser evil. They did not surround their policy with the dignity and the glory of justice. They did not impress the popular imagination and stimulate the popular reverence by the spectacle of a statesmanship that acted only on the principle of right. Men saw that their rulers did the just act, not because they themselves believed it to be just, but because they found it to be expedient. Men saw that whatever was demanded with force enough at its back was likely to be regarded as a demand which it would be expedient to grant. Catholic emancipation was yielded not as a matter of justice, but in deference to a pressure from without which the Duke of Wellington declared that he could not resist. He said he had to choose between emancipating the Catholics and encountering a civil war, and he was not prepared to encounter a civil war. Even when emancipation was granted, and on these conditions, it was granted grudgingly. Every possible attempt was made to minimise its immediate influence. The man whose eloquence and energy had done more than any other influence to force emancipation on the Government, Mr. O'Connell, was kept out of Parliament as long as it was possible by any craft on the part of the Government to continue his exclusion. The effect of all this was to impress on the

English as well as the Irish people the conviction that
no justice could be had without a threat of violence, and
that anything could be obtained which was supported by
sufficient demonstration of strength. It is hardly too
much to say that to the manner in which the Government resisted Catholic emancipation, and their grudging
way of at last conceding it, is due a great part of the
discontent and disaffection which have existed in Ireland
from that time. It is clearly one of the defects of our
constitutional system, that a reform of any kind is seldom
made in mere obedience to the justice of the demand.
Perhaps this is a defect inseparable from a popular
system, and to be accepted merely as one of the disadvantages attending every organisation worked out by
men. The defect at all events is there, and its operation
may be observed in every chapter of our political history.
No matter how just may be the claims of a certain reform, no politician expects to see it granted spontaneously
and because of its justice. There must be agitation,
there must be popular clamour, there must very often be
something like a hint of possible resistance to the law
before the reform is carried.

Indeed, under our present system it is not easy to see
how the condition of things could well be different. The
House of Commons undertakes to manage the business
of the country. Every improvement of every institution
must be accomplished through its means. Each year
brings fresh demands for reform, and new development
in almost every direction. Anomalies which our fore-
fathers put up with good-humouredly and perhaps did
not even observe, are irritating and intolerable to us.
With the growth of education we become continually
more and more anxious to bring the practical working of
our systems into harmony with reasonable theories. All

our commercial and industrial systems require, in their gradual development, new changes of legislation to suit the altered conditions. Thus we find a multitude of voices crying out together for a change in some law. It is impossible that Parliament can undertake all the changes together, and it has therefore come to be understood that the reform which has the most and the loudest voices clamouring on its side must have precedence. It is a question not of the survival of the fittest but of the precedence of the fittest. Therefore, the course of legislation in our times is almost certain to go through successive stages each one of which can be foreseen and speculated on by prudent persons in anticipation. The reform is first discussed and justified by writers and thinkers. At this stage of its history Parliament cares nothing about it. Then it becomes a subject of agitation out of doors. When it has made stir enough in that way it becomes a question of Parliamentary debate. Parliament however for a long time takes no further account of the proposed reform than to have a discussion on it every session. Suddenly, however, by chance or otherwise, it grows strong with the country. Great meetings are held; stormy crowds come together; perhaps there are riots; at all events there is danger of public disturbance, and then at length Parliament suddenly finds that it has to deal with a more vehement claimant than any other just then demanding to be heard, and yields to popular clamour what it never would have thought of yielding to justice. As Comte described all the intelligence of man as passing through its three distinct gradations of the supernatural, the metaphysical, and the positive, so we may describe English reform as passing distinctly through the three stages of the study, the platform, and the Parliament.

It is worth noting, too, that the manner in which the representative constitution of the House of Commons has been expanded has not thus far tended in any degree to make it more ready to take the initiative in legislation. Still, as before, it waits patiently until the voice of the country calls on it to act and tells it distinctly what it is to do, before venturing on any action. In no matter of any importance whatever, does Parliament attempt to take the initiative, or to anticipate the wants and wishes of the country. In the days just before the passing of the Reform Bill, the epoch with which we are now immediately concerned, it seemed to be the principal office of Parliament to resist as long as possible every public and popular demand. Statesmanship then appeared to have accepted, in domestic policy at least, the simple business of obstruction. To resist change so long as it could safely be resisted, was then apparently an English Minister's notion of his duty. Well was it for England that this was all that her statesmanship felt itself called upon to do. Statesmen in other countries believed themselves conscientiously bound to resist change even at the peril of national peace, to resist it to the death.

CHAPTER III.

THE LEADERS OF REFORM.

For a long time previous to 1830, there seemed to be no fixed rule in these countries for the selection of the towns to have representatives in the House of Commons. The principle in former times appears to have been that the Sovereign issued his writ to any town or place he chose to select. The King invited such a place to send a representative to advise him. The assumption was that he chose the places to be represented in accordance with their population and their importance, but it is almost needless to say that the power which the Sovereign assumed was exercised very often in the most arbitrary fashion. Habit came in many cases to make the arbitrary choice permanent and perpetual. Many places which had been tolerably populous when the Sovereign first invited them to send representatives to the House of Commons, lost their population and their importance and fell into actual decay. Yet the Sovereign continued to issue his writ and to invite those places to send representatives to Parliment. In some instances the places named actually ceased to be anything more than geographical expressions. The hamlet or village, or whatever it might have been, fell into ruin. There was no population. The owner of the soil was perhaps the sole resident.

The case of Old Sarum is famous. Old Sarum was a town in Wiltshire. It stood not far from where Salisbury now stands ; Salisbury is in fact New Sarum. It returned members to Parliament in Edward I.'s time and afterwards in the days of Edward III., and from that period down to the time of the Reform Bill, which we are now about to consider. But the town of Old Sarum gradually disappeared. Owing to the rise of " New Sarum," Salisbury, and to other causes, the population gradually deserted Old Sarum. The town became practically effaced from existence ; its remains far less palpable and visible than those of any Baalbec or Palmyra. Yet it continued to be represented in Parliament. It was at one time bought by Chatham's grandfather, " Governor Pitt," as he was called after he had been Governor of Madras, the owner of the famous diamond. It was coolly observed at the time that " Mr. Pitt's posterity now

have an hereditary right to a seat in the House of Commons as owners of Old Sarum, as the Earls of Arundel
have to a seat in the House of Peers as Lords of Arundel
Castle." Ludgershall in Wiltshire was another place
which continued to send members to Parliament long
after it had ceased to be a constituency. This was the
place which was offered up as a free sacrifice by its representative during the debates on the Reform Bill. Gravely announcing himself as the patron of Ludgershall, the
constituency of Ludgershall, and the member for Ludgershall, this gentleman declared that in all three capa-
cities he meant to vote for the disfranchisement of Ludgershall. A place called Gatton, with seven electors,
had two members. Two-thirds of the House of Commons was made up of the nominees of peers or great
landlords. The patrons owned their boroughs and their
members just as they owned their parks and their cattle.
One duke returned eleven members; another, nine.
Seats were openly bought and sold. In some instances
they were publicly advertised for sale. The poll might
remain open at one period for six weeks. In 1784 its
limit was reduced to fifteen days. Bribery, drunkenness,
hideous scenes of debauchery and riot went on without
intermission during all that time. A country or borough,
during a contest, was as completely surrendered to a
saturnalia of infamy, as a captured town used at one
time to be given up for a certain number of days to
the license of the conqueror's soldiery. Allowing for
the exaggeration permissible to a great humourist, it does
not seem as if Hogarth's famous picture of the election
gave any very extravagant notion of the things that
were done and the sights that were seen during a parliamentary contest in England. Public opinion had hardly
any influence on the choice of many, if not most of the

constituencies, even when there were constituencies to choose. Territorial influences and money settled the matter between them. While places no longer marked on the map had any representatives, the great manufacturing towns, such as Manchester, Leeds and Birmingham, were without representations. They had grown up to be prosperous and populous communities while Gatton and Old Sarum were sinking into decay and death, but the Sovereign's power to summon representatives did not deign to take account of them. In Ireland and Scotland the condition of things was on the whole still worse and more anomalous, if that were possible, than in England.

The franchise, both in counties and in boroughs, was so high as to preclude anything like the possibility of popular representation. On the other hand, this high level of franchise was balanced in the boroughs and cities by a number of arbitrary franchises, conferred on what were called freemen, resident and non-resident: on forty-shilling freeholders, and on various associations or corporations of men; and these, connecting no moral or political responsibility whatever with the exercise of the vote, really tended only to give better facilities for corruption. Some of these antiquated and anomalous franchises only introduced into the constituency a class of persons who were completely at the service of the highest bidder. They sold their votes as the informers in certain days of the Roman Empire sold their testimony.

Meanwhile, great English populations were growing into importance in the manufacturing districts. Towns and cities began to arise here and there whose vastness, wealth, and intelligence surpassed anything that could have been represented by local communities in earlier days of the Parliament. Towns like Birmingham and

Leeds and Manchester and Sheffield began to have a public opinion of their own, interests of their own, ambitions and aspirations of their own. Very naturally they began to crave for some place in the representative system of the country. Reform schemes were brought forward every now and then, and came to nothing. Lord Chatham, in 1770, supported a motion made by the Marquis of Rockingham, in favour of Parliamentary reform, and pointed out that "the strength and vigour of the constitution" must reside, not "in the little dependent boroughs," but in "the great cities and counties." The American War interposed and diverted attention from the whole subject. In 1782 his son, William Pitt, moved for a Select Committee on the subject of Parliamentary reform. In 1785, when Pitt was Prime Minister, he made an attempt to amend the representation by taking from thirty-six small boroughs their right to return members, and endowing certain counties or populous places with the privilege. His scheme also included a provision for gradually extinguishing the franchise of boroughs which might have fallen into decay. This scheme, however, was negatived by a majority of 74. It is not likely that Pitt was much in earnest about the matter; he would have had a much larger following if it had been generally understood that he really meant reform. Then the French Revolution intervened. That revolution, however, in the first instance, did more to excite the enthusiasm of reformers than to arouse the alarms of those who were opposed to reform. Mr. Charles Grey, the friend and pupil of Fox, afterwards Earl Grey, whose stately eloquence still survives in the memory of living men, took up the cause of reform, and presented a petition from Sheffield, from Birmingham, from the city of Edinburgh, and various other places, praying for Parliamentary reform. The most important, however, of the petitions which Mr. Grey presented, was the famous Prayer from "the members of the Society of the Friends of the People, associated for the purpose of obtaining a Parliamentary reform." This remarkable petition, presented to the House of Commons on May 6, 1793, declared that no less than 150 members were actually nominated by members of the House of Lords; that 40 Peers returned 81 members by their own positive authority in small boroughs, and that an absolute majority of the Representative Chamber were returned by influences entirely independent of, and opposed to the representative principle. The petition also complained of the length and the cost of electoral contests, and of the complicated "fancy franchises" which we have already mentioned.

The House of Commons, whose constitution was challenged by this petition, decided by an overwhelming majority in its own favour. Then the wild days of the French Revolution interposed, and a reaction led by Burke's famous Essay set in amongst all the influential classes of English society.

Reform, the safeguard against revolution, became identified with revolution itself, in the minds of most men. The reform question fell into something like oblivion. Mr. Grey, indeed, raised the subject in Parliament once or twice, but each time apparently with less chance of success and with diminished favour. Not for some years after the fall of Napoleon, and the temporarily decisive victory of Waterloo, did the subject of Parliamentary reform become a serious question in the House of Commons. It was not allowed to lie wholly in abeyance all this time. Now and again a motion was brought forward in the House by Sir Francis Burdett, by Lord John Russell, by the Marquis of Blandford, by Lord Howick, son of Charles, now become Earl Grey, and by other men having the object of dealing with the question, or with some branch of it, but without any marked result.

Lord Grey was still the recognised leader of the reform party. He had been the friend and pupil of Fox. He was a man of remarkable energy and unbending character. Macaulay has paid a well-merited tribute of praise to the stately eloquence of which he was a master. In his younger days he had been one of the managers of the famous impeachment of Warren Hastings. He appeared side by side with Burke and Fox and Sheridan and Windham. "Nor," as Macaulay says, "though surrounded by such men, did the youngest manager pass unnoticed." "Those," adds the historian, "who within the last ten years have listened with delight till the morning sun shone on the tapestries of the House of Lords, to the lofty and animated eloquence of Charles Earl Grey, are able to form some estimate of the powers of a race of men amongst whom he was not the foremost." Lord Grey's eloquence was probably of a kind hardly known to our time. It seems to have been measured, stately, grand, better suited to illustrate great principles and advocate large reforms, than to deal with what we may call the mere business details which take up most of the work of Parliament at the present day. Although the pupil of Fox, Lord Grey does not seem to have caught from his master any of that spontaneous and impassioned eloquence which has been described by Grattan as "rolling in resistless as the waves of the Atlantic." Those, perhaps, among us who can remember the lofty, half-poetic oratory of the late Lord Ellenborough, with its diction apparently raised above the level of ordinary events and common debate, will have a better impression of the style of eloquence in which Lord Grey was distin-

guished.   Lord Grey was a man of the highest personal
honour and character.   Nature had not, perhaps, given
him any great force of will or power of initiative.   He
was therefore apt to be sometimes under the influence of
those immediately around him.   He was said, for example, to be very much under the control of his son-in-
law, Lord Durham.   But Lord Grey had the entire confidence of the reformers of England, and was in every
way a man fitted to stand between Sovereign and people
at a great political crisis.   He had the courage to tell a
Sovereign what it became the Sovereign's duty to do,
although the admonition might be distasteful to royal
ears, and he had the firmness not to allow himself to be
led away too far by the impatient demands of a reason-
ably dissatisfied people.

The reformers out of doors would probably not have
been sorry if Lord Durham's influence over his father-in
law had been even greater than it was reported to be.
Lord Grey was ready to give that opportunity to younger
men which the leader of a political party is not always
found considerate enough to allow, and his most Radical
colleague at that time was Lord Durham.   The fame of
Lord Durham has curiously faded and become dim in
our day.   He was a man of a 'masterful' character, to
adopt an expressive provincial word.   He was a bold
and earnest Radical, going much further in some of his
notions on the subject of reform than most of the professed Radicals of our own day would be inclined to do.
He had a strong and resolute will.   His temper was
overbearing, and often swept away his judgment in its
fitful and sudden gusts.   He was too sensitive for his own
happiness or his success as a politician.   Lord Durham's
political career was short.   He had been long out of
politics when he died in the July of 1840, and he was

then only in his forty-ninth year. But at the time we are now describing he was the hope of all the more advanced Radicals of the country, and he had still a great career before him. It is fairly to be called a great career, although it was a failure so far as Lord Durham's political advancement was concerned. Lord Durham was sent out to settle the disturbances in misgoverned and rebellious Canada; and he founded the great, prosperous, self-governing country, in whose fortunes and progress we all now take so deep an interest. He evolved order out of chaos. He acted for the time as a dictator. He had to reorganise a whole country, and he did so without much regard for the sort of system which bungling legislation had tried in vain to establish. He was recalled; he was officially disgraced; but he might fairly have said that he had saved Canada. A Durham sent to Ireland about the same time, and allowed to follow out the guidance of his genius and his free political principles, might have unravelled the tangled work of blundering centuries, and made the basis of a thorough and cordial co-partnership between England and Ireland to endure forever.

Among the chiefs and captains of reform in those days there was one more widely popular, and even more strenuously self-asserting, than Lord Durham. This was Henry Brougham, soon after to be Lord Chancellor. Brougham was unquestionably the most energetic reformer of the period. His talents were miscellaneous, brilliant, and his capacity for labour seemed inexhaustible. He delighted in work. He seemed only to live and enjoy himself in work. Even his relaxations were of an eager, exhaustive kind. He had tremendous physical strength, great animal spirits, and an unlimited belief in himself and admiration for himself. It was impossible not to admire his genius, and not sometimes to laugh at his vanity. He was a great popular and par- liamentary orator. His style was too rugged, and at the same time too diffuse, for a time like ours. His passion would now seem to us like that of a madman; his action and his gestures would be intolerable to our Parliament. He sometimes seemed to foam at the mouth in the fury of debate, and on one occasion at least he went through the form of dropping to his knees in order to make his appeal to the Peers more impressive. At the time of which we are now speaking, he filled a vast space in the public mind. Untiring, restless, insatiable of praise, greedy of power, capable of commanding a public meet- ing almost as completely as O'Connell, he naturally be- came a powerful force in the promotion of great political and social reforms. He had rendered immense service to the cause of liberty and to that of education. He had been the most uncompromising enemy to the system of slavery in the colonies. It was his voice which denounced "the wild and guilty phantasy" that man can have pro- perty in man. He was a law reformer. He was one of the founders of what may be called popular education, and an advocate of religious equality. He threw himself for a time with all the wild, coarse, animal energy of his nature into the cause of political reform.

But the man who rendered the most decided service to the cause, and who, during the whole of his active career, was more distinctly identified with reform than any other statesman, was Lord John Russell. Russell was not a man of genius, and he never became an orator. But he had strength of character and of will, and he saw his way clearly before him. During the whole of his long career he was never turned aside by a personal motive from any principle of policy. He was a ready, keen, penetrating debater. The force of his cold, quiet sarcasm told irresistibly on any weak point in an opponent's argument. He had sat at the feet of Fox. He loved literature as well as politics, and was a personal friend of most of the great literary men of his time. Lord John Russell, more than any other man, kept the light of political reform burning during seasons when it seemed almost certain that it must go out altogether.

CHAPTER IV.

THE EVE OF THE REFORM STRUGGLE.

PARLIAMENT assembled on February 4, 1830. It opened under conditions of peculiar gloom. The Royal speech spoke of the general distress from which commerce and agriculture, and all the classes that depended upon either, were suffering. The speech, of course, did not do more than barely allude to the distressed condition of the time. The state of the working men in many parts of the country was little better than that of starvation. The best of the silk weavers were earning only an average of eight or nine shillings a week, and in some larger towns it was declared that many thousands of working people were receiving no more than 2½ d. a day, to say nothing of the large numbers who were out of employment altogether. Many of the working-men ascribed the depression in trade to the introduction of machinery, and there were organised gangs of workmen going through the country trying to break and destroy all machinery which they believed to interfere with their trade, They followed the example of the Luddites of an earlier day, who used to go about in bands, breaking frames and machinery, starting riots in various places, and coming into collision with the military, and of whom several were tried and executed from the year 1811 to 1818. The Luddites took their name from a silly creature, really an idiot, named Ludd, who had once broken some weaving machinery in a fit of passion. Perhaps the Luddites will be remembered by many persons in our time, rather because of Byron's allusion to them than by reason of any historical mark they have made. In December 1816, Byron wrote a little ballad, which he called the "Song of the Luddite," in which he declares that :

> As the Liberty lads o'er the sea
> Bought their freedom, and cheaply, with blood,
>   So we boys, we,
> Will die fighting, or live free,
> And down with all kings but King Ludd.

Byron wrote to Moore *àpropos* of this poem, asking "Are you not near the Luddites ? By the Lord, if there's a row, but I'll be among ye. How go on the weavers, the breakers of frames, the Lutherans of politics, the reformers ?"

The policy of the Luddites was foolishly followed out by some of the working-men in 1830. It is likely enough that the machinery did for the moment disturb their trade and interfere with employment, and men with wives and families suffering from starvation cannot be expected to have the patient temper of economists and philosophers. It is certain, however, that the outbursts of anger and violence tended only to make their condition more distressed and miserable, and that the machinery against which they protested was destined to multiply the operations of the trade and to give additional and vastly increased employment to numbers of men and women. The country was in such deep distress that Lord Stanhope

in the House of Lords, moved an amendment to the Address, stating that agriculture, trade, commerce, and manufactures had never before at any one time been in so disas-
trous a condition. The Duke of Wellington, on the other
hand, contended in the true fashion of the Minister of
State, that although there was suffering in some parts of
the country, yet on the whole the condition of things was
improving. It is hardly necessary to point out how
illusory an answer this is to a special appeal. There was
deep distress in certain parts of the country, which,
according to the argument pressed on the Government,
might be relieved by a wise system of commercial legislation. It was no answer whatever to such an appeal to
say that the country on the whole was more prosperous
than it had been before. It would be just as reasonable
if some complaint were made of the want of fire-
engines in a particular quarter of the town which had
lately been ravaged by a conflagration, to say that,
taking the country all over, the average of fires was less
than it had been for some years previous. In the House
of Commons Sir Francis Burdett denounced the Duke of
Wellington as " shamefully insensible to the suffering and
distress which were painfully apparent through the land."
O'Connell, in the course of the debate, declared that
many thousands of persons had to subsist in Ireland on
three halfpence per day. A tolerably successful working-
man sometimes got 2*s.* 6*d.* a week, and at this time the
four-pound loaf cost 10*d.* Sir James Graham suggested
a reduction in the salaries of Government officials. Mr.
Hume, true to the purpose of his life, proposed that
8,000,000*l.* should be saved from the expenses of the
army and navy. Mr. Poulett Thompson moved for a
Committee of Inquiry into the whole system of taxation.
Sir Robert Peel accepted none of these suggestions and

recommendations. The Ministry managed tolerably well in their financial measures, and contrived to have a considerable surplus to show. The early part of the session was marked, so far as political reform was concerned, only by Lord John Russell's introduction of a measure to give members to Manchester, Liverpool, and Leeds, and one introduced by Mr. O'Connell to introduce universal suffrage and vote by ballot. Both these measures were rejected.

Nothing could well have seemed gloomier than the prospect of popular reform in England. The most earnest and courageous of the reformers must have felt their spirits sink within them as the early months of 1830 went on. The unforeseen, however, then as in other cases, came to pass. Just at the moment when the light seemed on the point of dying out, events occurred which combined to set it suddenly aflame again, more brightly than ever. The first of these events was the death of George IV. on June 26, 1830. George had begun his public life as an avowed Whig. He was a friend and boon companion of Fox and Sheridan. It is certain that Fox and Sheridan believed him to be their close political ally as well. There was in fact a Prince's party in the State. The Prince of Wales was believed to be the direct opponent of the policy favoured and enforced by the King. The Whig millennium was looked for when George should succeed to his father's throne. It was in his eagerness to have George made Regent during his father's first attack of insanity that Fox actually propounded the doctrine that the Prince of Wales was entitled to become Regent independently of any decision of Parliament. This strange profession of political faith caused Pitt to declare in exultation that he would " un-Whig " the gentleman for the rest of his life. Fox, indeed, had for the moment been betrayed into a repudiation of one of the first and most essential principles of Liberalism. No wonder that his great rival exulted.

George had given new hope to Ireland, and was at one time all but adored by the Irish people. Moore sang his praise and O'Connell glorified him, at the time when Byron was heaping unmeasured scorn on him in "the Irish avatar." Byron himself, indeed, had once believed in the Prince. Moore afterwards denounced him bitterly in song. George disappointed others as well as Moore. Once before he had turned suddenly against the Whigs, and separated himself publicly and formally from them. In May, 1792, he delivered in the House of Lords a speech in which he announced that he could not accept the views on the French Revolution which Fox and his friends still continued to hold. There was after this a renewal more than once of the friendly relations between the Prince and Fox, and the hopes of the Whigs were drawn to the Prince Regent again. It was long after this that Fox, in his eagerness for the Prince, laid himself open to the rebuke of Pitt, and it was still later, and after he had become king, that George revisited Ireland. But from the moment when the Prince became Regent he showed that the Whigs had nothing to expect from him, and in his reign as Sovereign he held distinctly and doggedly by the principles and the political creed of the Tories. George has left a poor name in English history. His vices were many; his virtues few. But it is not perhaps sufficiently borne in mind that he was kept in a pitiful state of pupilage by his father's orders during years that almost approached to manhood. His life was spent up to about the age of eighteen in a sort of scholastic imprisonment, now in Windsor, now in Kew, and now in Buckingham Palace. He was treated by his father very much as Joe Willett, in "Barnaby Rudge" is treated by Old John. Joe Willett, however, could run away and George could not; and Joe Willett had a noble nature and George certainly had not. But it is only right to point out that the career of George, on his emerging at last from *duresse*, was not very unlike what reasonable men would have looked for as the result of sudden license after long and undue restraint.

Everyone had come to know that reform had no chance while George IV. lived. When he died, therefore, the hopes of the reformers sprang up anew. William IV. succeeded, and although William had strongly opposed Liberal policy and Liberal principles in many important questions, yet it was considered that he came to the throne unpledged on the subject of Parliamentary reform. It was hoped that he would be glad to renew the popularity of his early days, and it was presumed that the influence of public opinion could not be without some effect on his reign. The Duke of Wellington and Sir Robert Peel were the leaders of the Ministry when George IV. died. "The Sailor King," as he was called, was thought to be of a genial and conciliatory disposition, and it was supposed that men of more progressive political opinions than Wellington or Peel might have some chance of influencing his public conduct.

Parliament was dissolved, by proclamation, on July 24, 1830. The Liberals went to the country full of hope and spirit, although they little dreamed that an event which was about to happen in another land was destined to give a new and most important impulse to the cause which they had at heart.

It might be thought that men whose principles were so poorly represented among the constituencies could have little hopes from the general election. But at all

times, even under the narrowest suffrage, it is certain
that in a country like this a strong public feeling exercises some control over the votes of the electoral body.
No matter how great the influence of landlords and local
magnates, no matter how vast and lavish the bribery and
corruption, yet a vigorous breath of public opinion does
in some manner contrive to force its way into the electoral body, and to impel them in the direction which the
popular sentiment is taking. Besides, it must be owned
that so far as territorial influence and influence of money
went, the Whigs of that day were not ashamed to compete, as far as possible, with their opponents. The state
of the franchise in the great towns, as we have already
explained, left the constituency peculiarly open to the influences of bribery, and there can be no doubt that the
Liberals, whenever they had a chance, availed themselves of the opportunity thus given. At all events, the
two parties were not so entirely disproportionate in
strength as the condition of things might lead a reader to
expect.

Suddenly, however, the unlooked-for event occurred
which turned the balance in favour of the Whigs, and
roused a popular feeling all over the country which the
narrow electorate found it difficult to resist. This event
was the Revolution of 1830 in France. Everyone who
studies with any attention the history of England, and
especially of political and Parliamentary movements in
England, will have observed the remarkable manner in
which events in this country follow the lead of events on
the Continent. If there were direct electrical or magnetic
connection between Continental Europe and the English
public mind there could hardly be a more direct connection between events on this side of the Channel and
events on the other. Revolution on the Continent always

in the first instance impels the cause of popular agitation in
this country. Then, it may be, the revolution goes too far,
and reaction sets in here for a time. Reform is dreaded
and detested, and men think they can hardly go far
enough back in the opposite direction. Then, again, it
may be that the wildness of the revolutionary movement
subsides in France, or in whatever Continental countries
it dominates. Institutions seem to emerge safer and
stronger than before from the welter of parties, and at
once a new effect is produced in England, and the popular movement receives a fresh impulse. The Revolution
in France took place because the French Ministry, disappointed at finding that each election produced a Chamber of Deputies more opposed to the arbitrary power of
the King and his advisers, and that the journals became
more and more outspoken in their condemnation of the
system of government, issued a body of ordinances,
changing practically the whole Constitution of the country, and superseding or destroying the liberty of the
Press. The French Ministry overdid their part. They
went far beyond any limit which the people of Paris
could tolerate. There was an insurrection for which the
Government were wholly unprepared, and after the famous struggle in Paris, known as the Three Days of
July, the King abdicated in favour of his grandson, but
abdicated in vain. The Revolution was complete so far
as the elder branch of the family was concerned. Charles
escaped to England. The white flag, the symbol of
French legitimacy, was flung away; the tricolor was substituted; the Duke of Orleans, Louis Philippe, became
King of the French, " King of the Barricades," as he was
afterwards called, and crowned his strange life of soldier-
ing, of exile, of school teaching, of wandering, by becoming for the time the most popular monarch of Europe.

This event promised to bring about an entirely new chapter in the history of France. The effect on English popular opinion was so strong, that after the general election the Tory Government found that it had lost at least fifty votes in the House of Commons, and that its influence all over the country was reduced to little better than a nullity.

CHAPTER V.

INTRODUCTION OF THE REFORM BILL.

THE new Parliament met on October 26, 1830. During the interval between the Revolution in France and the assembling of Parliament there had been many symptoms in England of a widespread popular discontent, and a determination to have some change in the policy of the Government. Incendiary fires alarmed many parts of the country in September and October, great public meetings were held in various cities and towns, and tumultuous demands were made for the dismissal of the Tory Ministers.

The actual work of the session began on November 2. On that day the King came to the House and delivered his speech in person. A debate arose in the House of Lords on the Address, and during this discussion the Duke of Wellington made his declaration with regard to parliamentary reform. Replying to a speech from Lord Grey, the Duke declared distinctly that he had never read or heard of any measure which could in any degree satisfy his mind " that the state of representation could be improved or be rendered more satisfactory to the country at large than at the present moment." " I am fully convinced," he said, " that the country possesses a

legislature which answers all the good purposes of legislation, and this to a greater degree than any legislature
has answered in any other country whatever." He went
further. He declared that not only the legislature but
the system of representation possessed deservedly the full
and entire confidence of the country. He therefore declared plainly that he was not prepared to bring forward
any measure of reform. Not only, he said, was he not
prepared to bring forward any such measure, but: "I will
at once declare that, as far as I am concerned, so long as
I hold any station in the Government of the country, I
shall always feel it my duty to resist such a measure when
proposed by others."

The Tory Ministry from that moment became odious
to the people. Never before perhaps was an administration so unpopular in England. The " Patriot-King," on
the other hand, was extolled to the skies, as the most
hopeful Prince who had ever mounted the throne. The
Whigs now believed they saw their way to the over-
throw of the Tory Ministry, and the Ministry began themselves to feel that they could not long stand up against
the demands of the country. The end came about perhaps even sooner than they had expected. On November 14, Sir Henry Parnell, afterwards Lord Congleton,
brought forward a motion in the House of Commons for
the appointment of a select committee "to take into consideration the estimates and amounts proposed by His
Majesty regarding the civil list." The Government
strongly opposed the motion, but it was carried in spite of
their teeth by a majority of twenty-nine. The question
was hardly one of capital importance in itself, but the
Government foresaw that if they did not resign on that occasion they would probably be forced to surrender very soon
after on some subject of graver moment. They therefore

thought it wise to tender their resignation the morning after their defeat. Perhaps too they thought it would be a clever party stroke to resign after a defeat which seemed to exhibit them as champions and defenders of the royal prerogative in opposition to Whig assailants. At all events, they made up their minds to tender their resignation. The resignation was accepted, and the same evening both Houses of Parliament knew that the Tory Ministry had come to an end.

Lord Grey was at once sent for by the King and invited to form a Ministry. This was of course only what everyone expected. Lord Grey consented to take office on condition that the reform of Parliament should be made a Cabinet measure. Some difficulty arose during the arrangements about finding a position for Lord Brougham. Lord Brougham was the most powerful Whig orator in the House of Commons. He had a considerable number of followers of his own, and what with his great abilities and energies, and the strength of his popularity, he might have made it hardly possible for a Whig ministry to keep in power without his support or in spite of him. Some of the Whigs thought there was no living with him or without him. But at all events it was necessary to make the experiment of living with him, since living without him would have been manifestly impossible. Lord Grey offered him the place of Attorney-General, which Lord Brougham absolutely declined. Lord Grey suggested that he should be Master of the Rolls and remain still in Parliament, but to this the King objected. The Prime Minister pointed out to the King that he could hardly venture to carry on the Government if Lord Brougham remained in the House of Commons under the conviction that he had been ill used by the party. William then suggested that he should be Lord Chancellor, and Lord

Grey explained that this was what he himself would have been disposed to recommend, but that the King had refused to allow Lord Brougham to be appointed to the inferior office of Master of the Rolls. The King's objection, however, was reasonable enough. Events afterwards proved that if William had wished to disarm Lord Brougham the course taken was politic and wise. Brougham, as Master of the Rolls, was to have retained his seat in the House of Commons, and would have been a most formidable power there, either against the Ministry, or the King, or both combined. As Lord Chancellor he sank into a position comparatively uninfluential. He hesitated for a while about accepting the place, but at last he was persuaded into it by Lord Grey and Lord· Althorp.

Lord Grey of course was at the head of the new Government. Lord Durham was Lord Privy Seal. Lord Althorp became Chancellor of the Exchequer, and leader of the House of Commons. Lord Althorp was a plain, straighforward country gentleman, with a great taste for farming and no personal inclination for political life. He was not even a tolerably good speaker. But his plain, homespun ability, his straightforward manners, his sound judgment and his absolute disinterestedness made him a genuine power in Parliament. Perhaps the House of Commons has never had a leader in whom it placed a fuller confidence. Once in replying to some opponent, Lord Althorp remarked that the gentleman's arguments were plausible but unsound. "I do not," he said composedly, "recollect now the reasons which prove his objections to be groundless; but I know that those reasons were perfectly satisfactory to my own mind." Lord Russell, who tells the story, adds that "the House voted, by a great majority, against the

plausible arguments, and in favour of the unknown re-
plies." This assuredly was carrying confidence about as
far as devotion itself could bear it. Lord Melbourne was
Home Secretary, and Lord Palmerston entered for the
first time into that office with which his career and his
fame were afterwards especially identified—the office of
Secretary for Foreign Affairs. Lord John Russell was
Paymaster of the Forces, and had not a seat in the Cabinet. Mr. Stanley, afterwards Lord Derby, became Irish
Secretary. The Lord Chancellor for Ireland, Lord Plunket, was, as a parliamentary orator, at least the peer of
his English colleague Lord Brougham.

Immediately after Lord Grey had formed his Ministry,
Lord Durham asked Lord John Russell to call upon him
at his house in Cleveland Row. Lord Durham there
explained that Lord Grey wished him to consult Lord
John with respect to the formation of a committee to
draw up the outlines of a plan of political reform. After
some deliberation it was agreed to invite Sir James
Graham, then First Lord of the Admiralty, and Lord
Duncannon, Commissioner of Woods and Forests, to
form a committee for the purpose, with Lord Durham
and Lord John Russell. Lord Durham then asked Lord
John Russell to draw for the consideration of the committee, a sketch of the principal heads of the measure of
reform which he could submit to Lord Grey, and which
if approved by Lord Grey would be proposed to the
Cabinet. Lord John Russell himself, in his work, " The
English Government and Constitution," thus describes
the principle on which he proceeded in shaping a Reform
Bill. " It was not my duty," he says, "to cut the body of
our old parent to pieces and to throw it into a Medea's
cauldron with the hopes of reviving the strength and
vigour of youth." He made up his mind not " to deviate

from the tract of the Constitution into the maze of fancy, or the wilderness of abstract rights." "It was desirable, in short, as it appeared to me, while sweeping away gross abuses, to avail ourselves as far as possible of the existing frame and body of our institutions. Thus, if the due weight and influence of property could be maintained by preserving the representation of a proportion of the small boroughs with an improved franchise, it was desirable rather to build on the old foundations than to indulge our fancy or our conceit in choosing a new site and erecting on new soil—perhaps on sand—an edifice entirely different from all which had hitherto existed." But Lord John Russell goes on to say that at the same time he was deeply impressed with Lord Grey's conviction that none but a large measure would be a safe measure; "that to nibble at disfranchisement and cramp reform by pedantic adherence to existing rights, would be to deceive expectation, to whet appetite, and to bring on that revolution which it was our object to avert."

Lord John Russell accordingly drew up a plan which he presented to Lord Durham, and on which Lord Durham noted certain amendments of his own. Lord John Russell, in the introduction to his "English Government and Constitution," publishes his sketch of a reform bill. It was written on a single sheet of letter paper, and is reproduced with Lord Durham's original corrections, erasures and alterations. The first paragraph proposes that fifty boroughs of the smallest population according to the census of 1821 should be disfranchised. Lord Durham writes "approved" across this clause, and adds in the margin, "this would disfranchise all boroughs of fourteen hundred inhabitants." Clause two proposes that fifty more of the least considerable should send in future only one member to Parliament. This also Lord

Durham marks with approval, and writes in the margin, "this would apply to boroughs of three thousand inhabitants." Clause three proposes that persons qualified to serve on juries should have the right of voting. This clause Lord Durham strikes out. Clause four recommends that no person should vote in cities or boroughs, except in the city of London, Westminster and Southwark, unless he is a householder rated at 10*l.* a year, and had paid his parochial taxes for three years within three months after they became due, and had resided in the city or borough for six months previous to the election. On that clause Lord Durham makes no remark. Clause five proposes that eighteen large towns shall send members to Parliament, that the unrepresented parts of London shall send four or six additional members, and that twenty counties shall send two additional members each. All this Lord Durham approves. Clause six gives the right of voting in the new towns to householders rated at 10*l.* a year, or persons qualified to serve on juries. Lord Durham strikes out the jury qualification. Clause seven gave to copy holders and leaseholders having an interest of more than twenty-one years a right to vote in the counties. This Lord Durham approves. Clause eight relates to the poll to be taken in the hundreds of divisions of counties; clause nine to the closing of the poll in cities and boroughs on the second day. Clause ten proposes that no new right of voting shall be acquired in counties by any property of less value than 10*l.* a year. This tenth and last clause Lord Durham strikes out. The Committee discussed the right of voting for boroughs and agreed that it should be uniform, their opinion being that the freemen and the scot and lot voters (a class of persons who paid rates not on the same scale as their wealthier neighbours, but were rated

E

in proportion to their means) had, in process of time, become generally either dependent or corrupt. They endeavoured to find a qualification which should give the vote to the greatest number of independent men, and yet be as nearly as possible an equivalent for the old household right of voting of the seventeenth century, and this qualification they believed they had arrived at when they fixed the borough franchise at 10*l*. At one of the last sittings of the Committee vote by ballot was introduced into the scheme, we believe at the suggestion of Lord Durham, and adopted by the Committee; this proposal was afterwards omitted by the Cabinet, and it had been strongly opposed in the Committee by Lord John Russell. Thus altered, the plan, approved by Lord Grey, was adopted by the Cabinet. Lord Grey submitted it to the King, by whom, says Lord John Russell, " it was readily and cheerfully sanctioned."

The ministerial secret was well kept. It was thought to be of great importance that the enemies of all reform should not know what the Government had to propose until the moment came for introducing the scheme to Parliament. More than thirty persons were in the secret, and yet so much discretion was shown by all that not the faintest whisper of the contents of the Reform Bill got out before the hour of its actual presentation to the House of Commons. The Bill was introduced on Tuesday, March 1, 1831. Lord John Russell had been specially selected by the Government to introduce the Bill, because of the perseverance and ability with which he had advocated the cause of reform. It is worthy of notice that Lord John Russell not only introduced the Reform Bill, but was the first to adopt the name of Reformer as the designation of his own party, and to recognize the existence of the word Conservative as a description of the opposite school. The first of March was a day of intense excitement and even tumult in the House of Commons. Never before in that generation had there been so great a crowd of persons eager to get places in the House. Every inch of available space was occupied long before the business of the House began. When the doors of the various galleries were opened there was struggle, clamour, and confusion such as we generally associate with the gallery entrance of a theatre on Boxing-night. Indeed, it required a threat from the Speaker that he would have the galleries cleared before order could be restored and silence obtained. Then there was a further wrangle among the members themselves, some complaining that their seats, although marked with their cards, had been taken by others.

At last Lord John Russell's time came. He began his speech in a low voice amid profound silence. He never was an orator capable of commanding the emotions of a large and popular assembly. His manner, even at its best, was cold and inanimate. On this occasion he was naturally made nervous by the task he had before him, and he is described as having spoken for the most part in a lower tone and with less animation even than was usual with him. Lord John Russell explained that the Ministry wished to take their stand between two extreme hostile parties, neither agreeing with the bigotry of those who would reject all reform, nor with the fanaticism of those who would admit only one plan of reform. He showed that at an early period the ancient constitution of the country recognized fully the right of popular representation, and that a statute had provided that each county should send to the Commons two knights of the shire, each city two burgesses, and each borough two members. This practice, however, fell into disuse;

innovations and alterations crept in which all operated
against the representative principle, and though at the
early period to which Lord John Russell referred the
House of Commons, as he explained, did represent the
people of England, there could be no doubt that the
House of Commons as it existed in March, 1831, had
long ceased to have any really representative character.
One passage in Lord John Russell's speech was very
remarkable, and has often been quoted. He assumed
the case of a stranger arriving in England, finding it un-
equalled in wealth, and enjoying more civilization and
more enlightenment than any country before it, finding
that it prided itself on its freedom, and on its representatives elected from its population at stated periods to act as
the guardians and preservers of that freedom. He describes the anxiety of this stranger to know how the people
formed and secured their representation and chose their
representatives. "What, then, would be his surprise,"
Lord John Russell said, "if he were taken by the guide
whom he had asked to conduct him to one of those
places of election, to a green mound and told that that
green mound sent two members to Parliament? or to be
taken to a stone wall with three niches in it, and told
that those three niches sent two members to Parliament?
or if he were shown a green park with many signs of
flourishing vegetable life, but none of human habitation,
and told that that green park sent two members to
Parliament?" He then went on to say : " If this stranger
were told all this and was astonished at hearing it, how
much more astonished would he not be if he was to see
large and populous towns, full of enterprise, and industry, and intelligence, containing vast magazines and
every species of manufacture, and were to be told that
these did not send any representatives to Parliament?"

Lord John Russell therefore proposed to deal with three chief grievances ; first, the nomination of members by individuals ; second, the election by close corporations ; and third, the expense of elections. He proposed to deprive certain extinct and nominal boroughs of the franchise altogether. Every borough which in 1821 had less than 2,000 inhabitants should lose altogether the right of sending a member to Parliament. No borough which had not more than 4,000 inhabitants should send more than one member to Parliament. By this means the number of the members would be reduced by 168. Then came the question as to the reorganization and extension of the franchise. Lord John Russell proceeded to get rid of various complicated franchises, such as the franchise for householders paying scot and lot, burgesses, capital burgesses, burgage holders, freeholders, freeman, pot wallopers, and various other devices. He proposed to simplify the franchise and make it homogeneous in principle. A vote was to be given to each householder in boroughs paying rates for houses of the yearly value of 10*l*. and upwards. Resident voters, under the old qualification, were, however, to be allowed to retain their right during life, but the qualification would expire gradually with the voters. In counties copyholders to the value of 10*l*. a year, qualified to serve on juries, were to have the vote. Leaseholders for not less than twenty-one years, whose annual rent was not less than 50*l*., were to enjoy the privilege also. The Government did not propose to fill up the whole of the 168 vacancies, as they believed that the House was already too large in its numbers. It was proposed that seven large towns should send two members each, and twenty other towns one member each. The seven towns to send two members were Manchester (with Salford), Birmingham,

Leeds, Greenwich, Wolverhampton, Sheffield, and Sunderland. The Metropolis, according to Lord John Russell's plan, was to have eight additional members, two to each of the following boroughs : Tower Hamlets, Holborn, Finsbury, and Lambeth. Each of the three Ridings of Yorkshire was to have two members, and twenty-six counties, in each of which the inhabitants exceeded 150,000, were to have two additional members. In order to meet the enormous expense of elections it was proposed that the poll should be taken in separate districts, so that no voter should have to travel more than fifteen miles to give his vote. In Scotland the suffrage was to be given to every copyholder to the annual value of 10*l.*, and to the holders of leases of ten years paying 50*l.* rent, Several towns were to have an increase in their representation, and thirteen districts composed of district boroughs, united for the purpose of representation, were to return one member each. In Ireland the right of voting was to be given to all holders of houses or land to the value of 10*l.* a year. Belfast, Limerick, and Waterford were to have representation. The number of persons who were to be entitled to vote under this Bill and who had no previous franchise were to be, in the counties about 110,000, in the provincial towns, 50,000, in London 95,000, in Scotland 50,000, in Ireland about 40,000 ; in all, half a million of persons were to be added to the constituency of the House of Commons.

The opposition to the proposals of the Government began at once. It is not usual in Parliament to debate much on the mere request of a Minister for leave to bring in a Bill, but on this occasion no one cared much to stick closely to precedent. Lord John Russell's motion was opposed by Sir Robert Harry Inglis, member

for the University of Oxford, a man whose curious parliamentary career is remembered even in our own time.
He was an intelligent man, a man of education, of strict
political integrity and honour, but he was opposed to any
kind of reform which took the direction of popular suffrage. He was opposed, indeed, to any change whatever
in the existing institutions of the country. We have
hardly any public man now who represents the kind of
political superstition which was illustrated in the honest
creed of Sir Robert Inglis. Change of all kind was to
him odious, nor could he see any wisdom in accepting
even an inevitable change. He insisted that reform
was only revolution. He insisted that Lord John Russell's Bill would destroy all the natural influence of
education, rank, and property. He went still farther.
He argued gravely that no such principle as that which
connects taxation and representation was known to the
English Constitution. He denied that there was any
idea whatever of the representative principle in the
political system of England. He insisted that no town
or borough had ever been called into parliamentary
existence because it was large and populous, or shut
out from it because it was small. The principle, he
said, on which Parliament was founded was that the
Sovereign should invite whomsoever he pleased to consult with him on the affairs of the country. He justified
even the purchase of boroughs, and insisted that if they
were not to be bought the noblemen of the country could
hardly be represented in Parliament at all. He defended
the small boroughs, the " close and rotten boroughs," as
they were called in the course of the debate, and contended but that for them Parliament would lose some of
its brightest ornaments. This argument, indeed, we have
heard repeated ·at a period much nearer to our own time,

and by a man of very different order of intelligence from
Sir Robert Inglis ; by no less a person than Mr. Gladstone himself. Sir Robert Inglis declared that a torrent
of mob oratory was a curse to the country, and was used
for the purpose of influencing the lowest and the most
debasing passions, and by "mob oratory" we may say
he meant any kind of eloquence used for the purpose
of asserting popular rights. Sir Charles Wetherell was
another representative of a political school which can
hardly be said to exist in our time. He went, if possible,
still further than Sir Robert Inglis in his opposition to
reform, but he had not Sir Robert Inglis's ability, and his
Toryism was more calculated to make the House laugh
than to make opponents angry.

Sir Robert Peel opposed the introduction of the Bill
on grounds more plausible and with better effect. He
declared that he cared not whether the House was dissolved or not, and that he should not consider himself
fit for the performance of a single legislative duty if he
permitted such a menace to influence him. He condemned those who had "excited the people to a pitch of
frenzy, and spurred their lazy indifference to an accumu-
lation of revolutionary clamour." Common prudence, he
said, would have forborne introducing a measure of the
kind at such a crisis in our foreign and domestic relations,
when causes of fresh excitement ought to have been
avoided. He insisted that "the inevitable tendency" of
the Bill would be "to sever every link of connection
between the poorer classes and that class from which
their representatives are usually chosen." In this one
argument we think there was some practical justice.
The tendency of the Bill was undoubtedly to leave the
poorer classes out of the representation altogether. The
abolition of the various "fancy franchises," then in exist-

ence, would remove the only chance which the poorer classes and the working classes in particular had of influencing the elections. Peel's argument in favour of the close borough system was based on a principle that we can easily understand. He pointed to the number of men who had entered the House for boroughs which the present Bill would disfranchise. Lord North, Burke, Pitt, Flood, Fox, Plunket, Canning, Windham, Huskisson, Brougham, Romilly, and several others were all first returned for close boroughs. When by caprice or want of money, or otherwise, some eminent men were deprived of larger seats they were rescued by some of the close boroughs, and their valuable labours thus secured to their country. Sheridan defeated at Stafford found shelter at Ilchester; Windham rejected by Norwich was received at Higham Ferrers; Lord Grey refused by Northumberland was accepted by Tavistock. This was the kind of argument with which England was made familiar in later years. It was an argument used by Sir Robert Peel's greatest pupil, Mr. Gladstone, against a further disfranchisement of small boroughs. It is plain, however, that any such advantage attaching to the existence of small boroughs is only one casual benefit to be measured against a great many certain and inevitable disadvantages. The close boroughs were nests of corruption, where they were not actually pocket boroughs and the property of some peer or landowner. Neither the system of corruption nor the system of nomineeship can be said to be creditable or endurable in a civilised country. Against these gross and monstrous defects we have to set off the single and chance advantage that a close borough, owned by an intelligent master, might sometimes be the means of returning an able man to the House of Commons. This is all that can be said in justification of the system, and it is not much to say. Besides, it is plain that with the growth of education, of independence, and of public spirit the close boroughs would lose entirely this preponderating advantage. As large and popular constituencies grow more enlightened and more independent they would show themselves not less willing to return distinguished men than the closest borough owned by the most liberal proprietor. In our own day, we see that men of talent, without family or wealth, have a much better chance, in the large and populous boroughs, than they would have in a small close borough the property of a peer or a landlord. Where the small borough was not the property of a peer or a landlord, it had of course no advantage ; for the class of voters who could be bought by the dozen for money and beer were not likely to be greatly impressed by the genius and the claims of some moneyless Sheridan or too conscientious Burke.

Sir Robert Peel's speech was answered by Mr. Stanley, afterwards Lord Derby, and answered very effectively as to that one point about the small boroughs. Whatever advantage, Mr. Stanley said, might be derived from that mode of admission would be more than counterbalanced by the disadvantage that the class of persons thus introduced, whatever their talents, would not be looked upon by the people as representatives at all. The debate was adjourned to Tuesday, March 8, and was then resumed by Mr. O'Connell. He gave the Bill his earnest support. There were, he said, objections to it. He declared that he himself was by conviction a Radical reformer, and that this was not a measure of Radical reform. " In every practical mode universal suffrage," he contended, " ought to be adopted as a matter of right." " The duration of Parliaments should be shortened to the time stipulated in the glorious Revolution of 1688, and above all, votes should be taken by ballot." It will now perhaps strike many persons as strange to find a man of Mr. O'Connell's country and faith describing the Revolution which unseated James II. and put William on the throne as the "glorious Revolution of 1688." But Mr. O'Connell was perhaps the last, as he was certainly the greatest, of the Irish public men whose political creed was on the whole identical with that of the advanced English Liberals. Another point in Mr. O'Connell's speech is worth noting. He contended that the representation of many parts of the country ought to be largely reorganized. He gave as an instance the fact that the population of Dublin amounted to considerably more than a fourth of the population of London, and that on that ground Dublin was fairly entitled to larger representation. The relative position of London and Dublin has marvellously changed since that time. Instead of being considerably more than one-fourth of the population of London Dublin is indeed considerably less than one-eighth. "When I hear triumphant assertions made," said O'Connell, "as to the working well of the present system, I would refer you to Ireland for an illustration. We have had a complete trial of it for thirty years at least, and yet Ireland is one of the most miserable countries on the earth, with wretchedness and starvation spreading desolation through the land

The debate went on during seven nights until an early hour of the morning of March 10. Lord Russell then replied. The Speaker put the question, "That leave be given to bring in a Bill to amend the representation of the people in England and Wales." The motion was agreed to without a division. The House of Commons seldom divides on a motion for the first reading of any measure introduced even by a private member, not to say a measure introduced by the Government. Leave was then granted to introduce Reform Bills for Scotland and for Ireland. It will easily be seen that the measures thus introduced must have fallen very far short of the wishes of advanced reformers. Everyone who pretended to the name of a Radical reformer and who took part in the debate expressed a certain sense of disappointment. We know that in the Cabinet, by which it was intrduced, there were influential members who would gladly have gone much further than Lord Grey or even Lord John Russell would have consented to go. The feeling of the country, therefore, was not one of very great enthusiasm at first. Perhaps if the Conservative leaders had been crafty, not to say prudent men, and had allowed the Bill to go through its various stages without serious opposition, the interest of the country would have diminished and languished, and it might have passed into law without arousing any feeling whatever. It ought to have been clear to the Conservative leaders that when once the Government of Lord Grey had proposed such a scheme there could be no quiet until that measure at least was carried, and that any decided opposition would only tend to inflame the passions and increase the demands of the people out of doors. Most of the moderate reformers in the country understood this perfectly well. They saw that nothing would satisfy the public, even for the present, short of the full provisions of the Bill as introduced by the Government. They dreaded lest, emboldened by the lack of popular enthusiasm, the Tory leaders should endeavour to defeat the Bill, and thus rouse public spirit into a passionate demand for some stronger measure. Therefore nearly all the leaders of popular movements out of doors lent what we may call a generous assistance to Lord Grey and Lord John

Russell. Their assistance was generous because the measure was not what they would themselves have proposed, and, indeed, in many points fell short of the scheme which a few months before they thought themselves entitled to expect at the hands of the Whig Government.

CHAPTER VI.

THE PROGRESS OF THE STRUGGLE.

On March 21, 1831, Lord John Russell moved the second reading of the Reform Bill. An amendment was moved to the effect that it be read a second time that day six months, and a debate took place which lasted two nights and was of a somewhat languid character, nearly all the great speakers of the House having already expressed their opinions and fully argued the question from all points of view. Three hundred and two members voted for the second reading, three hundred and one for the amendment, and the second reading was therefore carried only by a majority of one. The Opposition were for the time triumphant. They felt perfectly certain that a Bill which passed its second reading by only a majority of one could easily be so mutilated in Committee as to render it of little harm, even if it should succeed in passing through the House of Lords. When the Bill was about to go into Committee, General Gascoigne moved an instruction declaring that in the opinion of the House, " The total number of knights, citizens, and burgesses returned to Parliament for that part of the United Kingdom called England and Wales ought not to be diminished." Lord Althorp at once understood the meaning of this attempt. It was the first of a series of motions by

which the Opposition intended to interfere with the progress of the Committee in a manner which, as he said, if
submitted to would be fatal to the Bill, or at least so det-
rimental to it as to render it valueless.   When the House
divided there were 299 votes for General Gascoigne's
motion and 291 against it.

The majority against Government was therefore eight.
The Ministers made up their mind to appeal to the
country.   The King, it appeared, was strongly opposed
to a dissolution, and had intimated to his Ministers when
they first came into office that he did not feel inclined to
dissolve a Parliament so newly elected in order to enable
them to carry a Reform Bill.   Now, however, the Ministers were determined that Parliament should be pro-
rogued at once with a view to its speedy dissolution.
There was a great deal of trouble to induce the King to
consent to this arrangement.   On Lord Brougham fell
the disagreeable task of announcing to William the
advice of the Ministry.   Something like a scene is said
to have taken place.   The King made all sorts of tech-
nical objections to the dissolution of Parliament, and
even, it is said, went to the point of accusing Lord Grey
and Lord Brougham of something like high treason in
having made arrangements to call out the Life Guards
for the closing ceremony of prorogation.   At last, however, William was prevailed upon, and the dissolution
took place.   Sir Robert Peel was actually speaking, denouncing the Ministry with a vehemence such as he
hardly ever showed before or after in the whole course of
his career, when the knock of " Black Rod " was heard
to summon the Commons to attend at the bar of the
Peers and hear the prorogation announced.

The dissolution of the Parliament was celebrated by
reformers all over the country with the utmost enthu-

siasm. There were illuminations in London and in most of the great towns. At the West-end of London some of the anti-reformers who refused to put lights in their windows had their houses attacked and the windows broken. The Duke of Wellington was one of those who became in this way the victim of a popular demonstration. The windows of Apsley House which look into Hyde Park were broken. The shutters on that side of the house were kept closed for years and years after, and popular rumour had it that the Duke of Wellington refused to allow the windows ever again to be opened which the anger of the public had thus vehemently assailed. When the elections came on vast sums of money were spent on both sides. It is to be feared that bribery and corruption were almost as active and as flourishing on the one side as on the other. In nearly all the great towns the result of the election was in favour of reform. General Gascoigne, one of the members for Liverpool, the man whose "instructions" to the Committee had been the first cause of the dissolution, found himself driven out of his seat by an overwhelming majority. Nearly all the English county members were now pledged to reform. The transformation effected by the elections was as great as any ever witnessed even in our own days, when complete changes of power are familiar to us as the result of an appeal to the country.

In the new Parliament Lord John Russell and Mr. Stanley appeared as Cabinet Ministers. On June 21 the King opened Parliament. As he went down to the House of Lords he was received with immense enthu- siasm both without and within the walls of Westminster Palace. On June 24 Lord John Russell introduced a second Bill on the subject of Parliamentary Reform. Except for some slight alterations in detail the new Re-

form Bill was practically the same as the old. The
second reading was brought forward on July 4, and the
debate occupied three nights. Three hundred and sixty-
seven votes were given for the second reading and two
hundred and thirty-one against it, thus showing a majority of one hundred and thirty-six in favour of the
Government. The Opposition now made up their mind
to try what they could do by a process more familiar to
our days than to theirs, the device of Parliamentary obstruction. Repeated motions for adjournment were made,
on each of which a discussion and a division took place.
There was something ingenious in the device by which
the debate was kept up through the whole of the night.
For example, some member of the Opposition would
move "that the Speaker do now leave the Chair." On
the motion being lost it would be moved "that the debate
be now adjourned." That motion being lost, somebody
would again move that the Speaker do leave the Chair,
and so with alternations of motions for the Speaker to
leave the Chair, and for the House now to adjourn, the
whole night was passed through, and it was half-past
seven in the morning when exhausted members were
allowed to go home, only to assemble again at three
o'clock that day. Scenes of this kind were repeated
again and again. Week after week passed on while determined Conservatives were talking against time, and
were making use of the forms of the House with every
possible ingenuity in order to delay the passing of the
Bill. The same speeches in almost the same words were
made over and over again, on every point concerning
which a discussion could possibly be raised. Reformers
both in and out of Parliament began to be seriously
alarmed. It seemed not impossible that, if tactics of this
kind were pursued, the Government might find it out of

their power to carry through the Bill in any time during which Parliament could be expected to sit. The disfranchising clauses of the Bill gave immense opportunity for debate. As each rotten borough proposed for sacrifice came under consideration, opportunity was taken not only for defending the existence of that particular place, but for repeating all over again the arguments against any manner of reform, with which the ears of the House had been wearily familiar for months.

Time and the hour, however, run through the roughest day. The extinguishing of the condemned boroughs was accomplished at last. The struggle then began over the boroughs which were to be reduced from two members to one. The work of obstruction set in again. It was arranged and drilled by a systematised process of organisation. " There was," says Mr. Molesworth in his " History of the Reform Bill," "a regular division of labor in the work of obstruction, which was arranged and superintended by a committee, of which Sir R. Peel was the President." " In order to promote delay," says the same author, "the leaders of the Opposition stood up again, and again repeated the same stale statements and arguments, and often in almost the same words." Between July 12 and 27, Sir R. Peel spoke forty-eight times, Mr. Wilson Croker fifty-seven times, Sir C. Wetherell fifty-eight times. At last, however, on August 2, the disfranchising clauses were finally disposed of, and the house then went on to consider the third clause, which gave two members each to large towns previously unrepresented. A night was spent in resisting the claim of Manchester, Birmingham, and Leeds to have representatives in the House of Commons. Meanwhile, meetings were being held in London and throughout the country, urging on the Government not to give way, to fight against the obstruction to the very last, and to keep Parliament sitting as long as might be necessary for the purpose of carrying the Bill. An important meeting of the supporters of the Government was held at the Foreign Office, over which Lord Althorp himself presided, and at that meeting he declared that "the enemies of reform are miserably mistaken if they hope to defeat the Bill by delay." "Rather than abandon the Bill," he declared, " Parliament will be kept sitting till next December, or next December twelve months if necessary."

August 18 was a somewhat memorable day. The Marquis of Chandos moved an amendment on the 16th clause, with the object of giving a vote to any farmer occupying on his own account land at the rent of not less than 50*l.* per annum, without any reference to the condition of his tenure. Lord Althorp opposed the amendment, on the ground that tenants at will, upon whom Lord Chandos proposed to confer the franchise, were for the most part completely dependent upon their landlords. A considerable number, however, of the reformers themselves took a different view, and supported the amendment on the ground that to enlarge as much as possible the principle of enfranchisement was the object they had mainly at heart. The amendment was carried by a majority of eighty-one. The Bill passed through committee on September 7. The report was taken on Tuesday, 13th, and its consideration occupied several evenings. On September 19 the Bill was read a third time. One hundred and thirteen voted for the third reading, and fifty-eight against. The majority was fifty-five. The numbers on both sides were small, because the House did not expect a division so soon. The anti-reformers took it for granted that there would be a long debate, but as it happened very few of them were in their seats when the third reading was proposed. Every captain of the Opposition apparently expected that somebody else would be ready to begin the discussion. Only one chief of their band, Sir J. Scarlett, happened to be in his place, and he endeavoured to talk against time, but was frightened out of his design by the vehement shouts of " divide." He gave way at last, and the division was taken, to the surprise of crowds of Tories who came rushing up to prolong the discussion, and arrived only in time to find themselves too late.

The motion that "the Bill do now pass," gave them, however, an opportunity for a discussion of three evenings more. At five o'clock on the morning of September 22, the last division took place. Three hundred and forty-five members voted for the passing of the Bill, 239 against it, showing a majority of 106 on the side of the Government. The Bill, however, had still to go before the House of Lords. It was brought up on the evening of the 22nd to that House. Lord Grey moved its first reading. No discussion took place, and on October 3, Lord Grey moved that the Bill be read a second time. His speech appears on the testimony of all contemporaries to have been fully worthy of the great occasion. It was closely argumentative in substance, stately and eloquent in style. Especially impressive was the concluding portion, in which he appealed to the archbishops and bishops in the House not to assist a narrow majority in rejecting the Bill. He appealed to them to remember that if their influence should enable the opponents of reform to throw out the Government proposition, the prelates would then stand before the people of England as the enemies of a moderate and just scheme of reform. Lord Wharncliffe moved that the Bill be read a second time that day six months. The Duke of Wellington and

Lord Lyndhurst opposed the Bill; Lord Brougham supported it, with characteristic energy and power. The division took place on the morning of October 8, and there was found to be a majority of forty-one against the second reading. The whole work of a session in the Commons had been done in vain. The Lords interposed at the last moment, and there was an end of reform for that year.

Some, at least, of the peers must have felt the responsibility of the situation very deeply, and must have found their hearts sink within them as they left the House of Lords on the dawn of that morning in autumn, and were able to say to themselves that they had interposed between the English people and a moderate and yet popular scheme of reform. Passionate emotion spread over the country when the news went abroad. Tumultuous meetings were held everywhere. In many towns the shops were closed, and mourning bells tolled from the churches. "Run for gold," became the popular cry, and a run was really made upon the Bank of England which at one time caused great alarm. Vast crowds assembled along the street from Whitehall to the Houses of Parliament, cheering the reform leaders, and denouncing with furious execrations the members of either House who had opposed the Bill. The Duke of Newcastle, the Marquis of Londonderry, and several other peers were attacked by mobs, and were saved not without some struggle and some danger. The bishops were the objects of special detestation, and a cry arose everywhere for their expulsion from the Upper Chamber. Indeed, proposals for the abolition of the House of Lords became popular almost everywhere over the country. Riots took place at Derby and at Nottingham. Nottingham Castle, the seat of the Duke of Newcastle, who had

made himself specially odious as an opponent of the
Reform Bill, was burnt to the ground. One of the
innocent victims of the time was Mrs. Musters, once
celebrated as Mary Chaworth, Lord Byron's first love,
about whom he had written his poem "The Dream."
The house of Mr. Musters was set on fire. The fire was
not allowed to spread, and indeed was put out without
much trouble, but Mrs. Musters in alarm fled from the
house, and took refuge in a garden. Terror and the
chill air brought on a fit of illness, which ended shortly
after in her death. Belvoir Castle, the seat of the Duke
of Rutland, was attacked by a mob. Bristol saw a series
of riots, the like of which had hardly ever been witnessed
in this country before. Sir Charles Wetherell, one of
the most notorious opponents of the Reform Bill, was
Recorder of Bristol, and came down to hold an assize
court there. When he entered the city, the carriage
in which he sat was escorted by a large number of
special constables, but it was attacked by a crowd.
Stones were thrown, several of the attendants were
severely injured, and it was with no little difficulty that
Sir Charles was enabled to make his way into the hall
where the court was to be held. A series of riots began.
The rioters for a time gained the upper hand, and Sir
Charles Wetherell had to escape from the Mansion
House in disguise; had to climb over the roofs of the
houses near, and had to be smuggled out of the city as
quickly as possible. The troops were at last called out,
the officers and men behaved with great forbearance and
discretion, and the riot was at last suppressed, but not
before the Mansion House, the Bridewell, and some
other public buildings had been thoroughly destroyed.
In almost every cathedral town there was what might be
called a special disturbance. The unpopularity of the

bishops was broad and deep, and many of the fiercer spirits in every mob took the opportunity to urge an attack upon cathedrals and churches. Even the reform Government themselves came in for a certain share of the fury against anti-reformers. Some wild suspicion got about that there were divisions in the Cabinet as to the expediency of pressing the Reform Bill, and it was feared that Lord Grey might be induced to put off the reintroduction of the measure to some indefinite time. Lord Grey felt a little hurt at these suspicions, and on one or two occasions rebuked a public deputation with something like asperity. The whole condition of things was such that a very slight act of indiscretion, or even a very slight excess of zeal at an inopportune moment, among the leaders on one side or the other, might have led to something like a distinctly revolutionary movement.

How near England came at this time to the verge of actual revolution, will probably be never known with certainty. It is easy now, as we look back from a safe distance, to underrate the extent of the danger. We have grown so accustomed to stability in our political affairs, that it seems hard to believe in the imminence of revolution at a time so near to our own. Yet it is hardly possible to doubt that during the reform struggle, England was brought once or twice very close to revolution, and that the great leaders of the liberal party of the day were aware of the danger, and were making preparations against it. Some of the Liberal leaders must have begun to be afraid lest the King should ultimately resist the pressure of the Ministry and of the public. They must have asked themselves what course it would be their duty to take in such an emergency. If the King persisted in opposing the operation of constitutional principles, it would be practically to attempt a revolution. Were the great Liberal nobles of England to side with the King against the Parliament and the people, or to endeavour to take such action on behalf of the Parliament and the people as might anticipate the unconstitutional action of the Crown? The dilemma appeared not unlike that which was presented when Charles I. broke away from his Parliament. Some at least of the influential English nobles seem to have been inclined to cast in their lot with the Parliament and against the Sovereign in the event of the Sovereign proving faithless to the constitutional principles by virtue of which alone he held his crown. Many years afterwards it came out that there was a tentative sort of correspondence going on under the sanction, or at least with the connivance, of some of the Liberal leaders, the object of which was to make arrangements for the disposition of the army in the event of the King's unconstitutional action rendering a struggle inevitable. During the trial of the Irish state prisoners at Clonmel in 1848 evidence was called to prove the existence of a correspondence which undoubtedly showed that some influential reformers were prepared, should the necessity be forced upon them, to side with the Parliament and the people against the King, and that they were trying to secure in advance the co-operation of the great soldier, Sir Charles Napier. Meanwhile popular excitement everywhere was growing to the wildest pitch. O'Connell, the Irish leader, threw all the aid of his eloquence and his energy into the cause of English Reform. He once addressed a great meeting at Charing Cross, and pointing with his outstretched right hand in the direction of Whitehall Palace, he reminded his audience that there a King had lost his head. Why, O'Connell asked, had this doom come on him? The orator supplied the answer himself. "It was," said O'Connell, "because he obeyed the dictation of a foreign wife." The allusion to the supposed influence of the Queen over King William was taken up by the crowd with instant appreciation, and was cheered with a vehemence which gave new emphasis to its political meaning.

Parliament reassembled on December 6, 1831. The King in person opened the session. His speech announced that measures for the reform of the Commons would be introduced, and added that "the speedy and satisfactory settlement of this question becomes daily of more pressing importance to the security of the State and the contentment and the welfare of the people." On Monday, December 12, Lord John Russell rose in the House of Commons to ask leave to bring in his third Reform Bill. There were no very important differences between the new Bill and the former measures. Some slight changes, of little account to us at this distance of time, were introduced, and these on the whole were rather of a nature to moderate than to strengthen the character of the Bill. The Opposition struggled hard to have the second reading delayed, and made it a reproach to Ministers that whatever changes they had introduced into their measures had been borrowed from the Conservative side of the House. The second reading of the Bill was taken on December 18, a Sunday morning. There were 324 votes for the second reading, 162 against it; a majority of exactly 2 to 1. Parliament adjourned for the Christmas holidays. Much of the early part of the New Year was occupied in trying the rioters who had made disturbances throughout the country. They were severely dealt with in some cases. Four men were executed at Bristol, three at Nottingham. Parliament reassembled on January 17, 1832; on the 20th the House went into committee on the Reform Bill. The tactics of obstruction came promptly into play again. From January 20 to March 14, was occupied in this sort of opposition. The Bill got out of committee then, and passed its third reading on March 23, by a majority of 116. It was introduced into the House of Lords at once, and its second reading fixed for April 9.

The great question now was whether the Lords would give way. A small group of peers, led by Lord Wharncliffe and Lord Harrowby, came into considerable prominence at this crisis. They were called "the Waverers," because their political action oscillated backwards and forwards between the Ministry and the Opposition. They really held the balance of power in the House of Lords. The course that they might decide upon at any moment would settle for the time the fate of the Reform Bill. Lord Wharncliffe went so far as to admit that some sort of reform measure must be introduced, but he voted against the second reading of the former Bill because he declared he had still a hope that something more moderate might be introduced. The key of the difficulty, however, was held in the hands of the King. If he would merely give his consent to a large creation of new peers, Lord Wharncliffe and his waverers would most certainly never put the Government to the trouble of carrying such a measure into effect. They would never run the risk of having their House flooded with reforming peers. But this was exactly what the King was unwilling to do. He hoped that the Waverers would assist him in his desire to get a very moderate, and from his point of view, a very harmless Reform Bill introduced. So long as there was any hope of thus tampering with the constitution, he was determined not to give way to the urgent demands of the

Ministry. He would not authorise them to threaten a new creation of peers. When the Bill was brought into the House of Lords on April 9, the Duke of Wellington announced that he was as determined as ever to offer it an uncompromising opposition. He was indiscreet enough in his speech to declare that he did not believe the King himself wished for any such reform as the Bill proposed. He said he was fully persuaded that it was a mistake to believe that the King had any interest in that Bill, and was satisfied that if the King's real feelings were made known to the country, Lord Grey would never be able to pass such a measure. The Waverers, however, supported the second reading of the Bill, and it was carried by a majority of nine. The policy of the Waverers seemed still to be carried out in the spirit and almost in the letter. They had helped the Minister to pass the second reading, but by a majority so small as almost to allow the Opposition to feel fully confident that they could so mutilate it in committee as to render it practically worthless. When the House went into committee, Lord Lyndhurst led the Opposition, and moved that the consideration of the disenfranchising clauses should be postponed until the enfranchising clause had first been considered, so that instead of making enfranchisement a consequence of disenfranchisement, disenfranchisement might follow enfranchisement. The Waverers declared that they would go with Lord Lyndhurst. It may seem that the question was of little importance, and only concerned the order in which the various clauses of the Bill were to be taken by the committee, but Lord Grey now, as on a former occasion, promptly declared that the real question for him was whether the control of the measure was to be left in the hands of its friends and its promoters, or whether it was to pass into the power and guidance of those who were always its bitter and deadly enemies.

He declared that if Lord Lyndhurst's motion were carried, he would regard it as fatal to the Bill. Lord Lyndhurst persevered, and his motion was carried by a majority of thirty-five. Lord Grey at once moved the adjournment of the debate and the further consideration of the Bill until May 10. It was now clear that Lord Grey was determined to carry the measure by the assistance of the King, or to resign his office. The King at first refused to give his consent to the creation of a sufficient number of peers to insure the passing of the measure. Lord Grey tendered his resignation, and the resignation was accepted.

The wild commotion that spread all over the country alarmed for a while even the stoutest opponents of reform. The Duke of Wellington himself may have felt his heart sink within him. Utter commotion prevailed in the palace. The King sent for Lord Lyndhurst and begged for his advice. Lord Lyndhurst recommended that the Duke of Wellington should be sent for. The King endeavoured to prevail on the Duke to take the leadership of a new administration. The Duke did not see his way, and recommended that Peel should be invited to form a Government. Peel knew well that he could not maintain a Ministry, and he naturally and properly declined. The Duke of Wellington was once more urged, and, out of sheer loyalty and devotion to his Sovereign, he actually made the vain attempt to get together an anti-reform administration. It was only an attempt. It came to nothing. Before the game was fairly started it had to be given up. Nothing was left but for the King to recall Lord Grey to power and consent to the measures necessary for the passing of the Reform Bill. Meantime the perplexed King was openly denounced all over the country. When his carriage was seen in London it was surrounded by hooting and shriek-ing crowds. The guards had to take the utmost care lest some personal attack should be made on him. Lord Grey and Lord Brougham insisted, as a condition of their returning to office, that the King should give his consent to the creation of a sufficient number of new peers. The King yielded at last and yielded in dissatisfied and angry mood, a mood which was intensified when Lord Brougham requested that the consent should be put into writing. At last William gave way, and handed a piece of paper to Lord Brougham, containing the statement that "the King grants permission to Earl Grey and to his Chancellor, Lord Brougham, to create such a num-ber of peers as will be sufficient to insure the passing of the Reform Bill." When that consent had been given there was an end to the opposition. The Duke of Well-ington withdrew, not only from any part in the debates on the Bill, but even from the House of Lords altogether until after the Bill had been passed. The Waverers of course gave way. It would be no further use to oppose the Bill. Lord Wharncliffe spoke bitterly against it be-cause he evidently thought he had been outwitted, if not actually deceived, by the Ministry, but there was no fur-ther substantial opposition to the measure. The Bill passed through the Lords on June 4, and the Royal as-sent was given to the measure a few days later.

The House of Lords, in yielding without further struggle, settled a principle without which our constitu-tional system could now hardly continue to work. They settled the principle that the House of Lords were never to carry resistance to any measure coming from the Commons beyond a certain point—beyond the time when it became unmistakably evident that the Commons were in earnest. Since that day no serious attempt has been made by the House of Lords to carry resistance to the popular will any further than just such a period as will allow the House of Commons to reconsider their former decision. When the House of Commons have reconsidered their decision and still adhere to it, it is now almost as clearly settled as any other principle in our constitutional system that the House of Lords are then to give way and withdraw all further opposition. It may be stated in plain words, that were the House of Lords now to depart from this implied arrangement, some modification of our constitutional system, as regards the Upper Chamber, would be inevitable. Another question settled we may hope for ever by the pressure brought to bear upon King William, was that which concerns the influence of the Sovereign's own personal will in legislation. The King gave way to the advice of his Ministers on a matter of vital importance to the nation, and on which his opinions were opposed to those of the majority. He yielded, not to mere argument or to mere persuasion, but to actual pressure. It became thereby settled that the personal will of the Sovereign was no longer to be a decisive authority in our scheme of Government. That was, we believe, the last time when the question ever was tested. With the close of the reign of William IV. and the accession of Queen Victoria to the throne, ended that chapter of our history in which the personal will of the Sovereign made one of the conditions under which the country is to be governed. It is now satisfactorily, and we trust finally settled, that the Sovereign always yields to the advice of the Ministers. As in the case of the House of Lords so in the case of the Crown, it may be said that any departure from the well-established and well-recognized principle, could we suppose such a thing possible, would now lead beyond doubt to some important modification of our whole constitutional system.

Some alterations, as we have seen, were introduced into the reform scheme in the course of its long struggle through both Houses of Parliament. But its main features underwent no material change. To us, looking back on the Reform Bill from this distance of time, it seems that nothing could have been more moderate and even modest in its proposals. Not that the change effected by it was not great. It amounted in truth to something like a parliamentary revolution. But there were certain distinct objects necessary to be accomplished if Parliament was to remain any longer in harmony with the spirit of the country, and in a condition to deal with its political wants, and it is not easy to see how the change could have been effected in a more cautious and a more gradual way. What the Reform Bill actually did was to pass sentence on the system of close or nomination boroughs, to establish in practical working order the principle that the House of Commons was a representative assembly, bearing due proportion in its numbers and in its arrangement to the numbers and the interests of the constituents, and to extend the suffrage so as to enfranchise the great bulk of the middle and lower middle classes of the community. The Reform Act was indeed very far from bringing representation and constituency into anything like exact proportion, but it made a distinct advance in that way, and it established a principle which is left to be wrought into a more perfect system by future generations. The Bill was only a compromise, but under all the circumstances it could hardly have been anything else. Lord Grey and his colleagues might have brought in a very modest measure of reform, some such scheme as other reformers were frequently bringing forward during the long dull interval when the question was not occupying the attention of any Government. Such a Bill, however, would have been almost as difficult to pass as that which they at last succeeded in carrying into law. On the other hand they might have endeavoured to satisfy the demands of the more Radical members of the House of Commons and of Radicals generally out of doors, and introduced a measure at once bold and comprehensive which would have settled the question for many generations. But we doubt very much whether it would have been possible to carry such a Bill just then. Certainly it would have involved the risk of a most serious struggle, perhaps of something like a warfare of class against class. Lord Grey attempted no uprooting of ancient institutions, and he carried with him what may be called the common sense and common instincts of the great bulk of the English population, in proceeding strictly on what were since his time called the old lines of the constitution. But it is certain that the Bill disappointed a great many not only outside the House of Commons but within it, and we may add not only outside the Government but even in the Cabinet itself. Its one main defect, as will afterwards appear, was the manner in which it left the great body of the working classes entirely outside what was called the pale of the constitution. It redeemed the political power of the State from being the monopoly of one great class, and made it the partnership of two great classes. That was an advance in itself, and it established the principle which made further advance possible. But it disappointed those who found themselves not better off but even worse off as regards the franchise than they had been before.

It is clear that the Bill was above all things one which it would have been wise on the part of the Conservatives to accept with as little resistance as possible.

It was the most moderate measure of reform which it was possible for any really reforming government to offer, or which would have been accepted by the people at large. It ought, one would think, to have been clear even then to an intelligent Conservative, that the country would never again be content to listen to any smaller project of reform. Yet the Conservatives had not the slightest idea of accepting any compromise. On the contrary, they had strong hopes that they would be able to resist the whole reform movement and beat it back. There were Tories who not only believed that the Government would never be able to carry any Reform Bill, but were even satisfied that the leaders of the Government did not expect to succeed. Sir James Graham was spoken to by a member in the lobby on the night after the first Reform Bill had been explained. The member who addressed him complimented him and his colleagues on their courage and honesty, but added that he supposed of course they were perfectly prepared to go out of office the next day.

In the course of one of the closing debates on the Reform Bill in the House of Commons, Lord John Russell made use of certain words which were often afterwards cited against him. They were quoted by extreme reformers to his reproach, and they were quoted by extreme opponents of reform as a Ministerial pledge against further change. Lord John Russell said, that in his opinion " so far as Ministers are concerned, this is a final measure. I declared on the second reading of the Reform Bill that if only a part of the measure were carried it would lead to new agitations, but that is now avoided by the state in which the Bill has come from the other House." It was instantly assumed by the extreme advocates of reform that Lord John Russell meant by these words to express his opinion that the era of reform had closed in England, that enough had been done in the way of change for all time, that the political system of this country was then the good made perfect. On the other hand, when many years after Lord John Russell undertook further schemes of reform, the extreme opponents of change accused him of having broken a solemn pledge. The speech was constantly referred to as Lord John Russell's " finality " declaration, and indeed the noble Lord himself was irreverently dubbed by certain critics, " finality Jack." The meaning, however, of Lord John Russell's statement is perfectly obvious, nor was there anything in it inconsistent with his taking up further schemes of reform at a distant period. What he meant was that as regarded that particular chapter of reform, Lord Grey's government felt that it had closed. They had done enough for the time. They knew very well that in English politics reforms are made in eras or in sections, and that the country will not stand the making of fresh changes year after year. The habit of the English people is to lay in a stock of reform which they believe will last a certain time, and to have no more to do with the question until the time seems to have nearly run out. Any practical politician would have seen that no matter how great might be the class grievances left unremedied by the Reform Bill of 1832, it would be impossible to induce Parliament and the public to set about a new scheme of reform immediately after. Lord John Russell meant, therefore, as indeed he said in plain words, that the government of Lord Grey regarded themselves as having done their part in the settlement of reform, and that having accomplished so much they did not propose to attempt anything further. Lord John Russell it seems almost needless to say, continued to be as steady an ad-

G

vocate of reform, after the passing of Lord Grey's Bill, as
he had been before. He knew well that the Bill was but
a beginning and a compromise, and that much more remained to be done even in his own time. He could not
be supposed to shut his eyes to the fact that that artisan
class, with whom he had always shown much sympathy,
were not only still left out of the franchise, but were, indeed, deprived of special franchises and political privileges which they had before the passing of the Bill. No
one of Lord John Russell's political sagacity could have
failed to see that the enfranchisement of the working class
would become a "burning question" before many years
should have gone over the heads of statesmen.

With the passing of the Reform Bill, the name of
Lord Grey may be said to pass out of history. He
had done his own special and appointed work, and
had done it patiently and well. It was a great effort on
the part of a man of his aristocratic descent, and somewhat cold and haughty temperament, to interest himself
so deeply and risk so much in a movement to extend the
franchise to a class of men with whom he could have had
but an imperfectly developed sympathy. His is not
a great figure in history, but it is a dignified and stately
figure. It represented a great movement, of which he
was not indeed the source and the inspiration, but of
which he was the successful guide and the graceful, imposing figure-head. His life links together two distinct
eras of our history, which but for that connecting bond
would be completely sundered. Lord Grey began his
political career as the friend and the associate of that
great group of statesmen and orators of whom it is not
too much to say that as a group they had not their rivals
in the previous history of England, and that they have
not found their rivals in the history of later days. We have

had since that time, as we had before, many great names, names in themselves perhaps as great as any which were shining in the early part of Lord Grey's career. But there was not before his time, and there has not been since, any group of statesmen who could be compared with the two Pitts, with Burke, with Fox, with Sheridan, and with Windham. Amongst such men Lord Grey did not indeed hold a commanding place ; but he was admitted into their company, he was looked upon as one of them, and some of their lustre is still allowed to shine over his more modest personal fame.

CHAPTER VII.

BLACK AND WHITE SLAVERY.

THE period which succeeded the passing of the Reform Bill was one of immense activity and earnestness in legislation. During the ten years of the Whig administration from 1831 to 1841—for we may take it as a whole period, notwithstanding one or two small breaks already mentioned or still to be mentioned—there were more plans and projects of reform in all directions set on foot and carried through than in any previous period of English history or in any subsequent period, if we except the marvellous three or four years of Mr. Gladstone's first administration. The first great reform was the complete abolition of the system of slavery in the British colonies. The slave trade had itself been suppressed so far as we could suppress it long before that time, but now the whole system of West Indian slavery was brought to an end. Despite the most gloomy prophecies on the part of lovers of the old system, despite the elaborate and exhaustive arguments that free labour never could compete with slave labour, and that the actual ruin of our sugar-growing colonies must be the result of abolition, the Government, driven on by public opinion, persevered and put an end to slavery in our colonies.

A long agitation of the small but energetic anti-slavery party brought about this practical result in 1833. In many parts of the colonial empire of Great Britain, especially in the West India islands, England had succeeded to the inheritance of a slave system and of an immense number of negro slaves. Granville Sharpe, Zachary Macaulay, father of the historian and statesman, Thomas Fowell Buxton, Wilberforce, Brougham, and many others had for a long time been striving hard to rouse up public opinion to the abolition of the slave system. The slave owners were strongly represented in Parliament. The idea that it was incumbent on any nation to abolish a slave system which they found in existence was something new to the public in general. The slave trade had already been abolished, not without many struggles and much difficulty, but the slave trade seemed to most persons to involve entirely different moral and economical principles from those which attached to the system of domestic slavery. To many intelligent and conscientious men it seemed quite reasonable to say that England should not allow a trade to go on in the forcible abduction and importation of unfortunate negroes from their homes in Africa, but they did not see that anything like a moral obligation rested upon England to abolish at a stroke a system of domestic slavery which had grown up in her colonies independent of any action of her own, which she found existing there, which had come down from almost all time, and which many or most of them believed to be not only necessary for the development of colonial interests, but for the advantage

and protection of the slaves themselves. Some three-
quarters of a million of slaves would have to be converted into free labourers in order to satisfy the appeal which
Granville Sharpe and Wilberforce were making.

Fowell Buxton was in Parliament. Zachary Macaulay
had resigned the management of a West Indian estate
because of his detestation of the slave system, and had
taken a leading part in promoting an attempt to found a
new negro colony at Sierra Leone, an attempt which
ended in failure. He was a man who thoroughly understood the condition of the slave colonies, and he was able
to furnish Buxton with a mass of hard facts which were
of immense influence in arousing public opinion in England. The most terrible disclosures were made as to the
brutal treatment of the negroes. For a long time the
slave owners had met every argument for emancipation
by insisting that it would necessarily be followed by a
negro insurrection, that the colonies would be exposed to
the most terrible danger, and above all, that the slaves
were treated with consideration and affection, such as
free labourers hardly ever received in England itself.
All the stories vaguely floating in England about the flogging of negro men and women, the branding and muti-
lations, were treated as absurd fables and were described
as such with the overbearing authority of the men who
have been there, and ought to know. The facts which
Zachary Macaulay assisted Buxton to collect put a stop
to this comfortable way of dealing with the question. It
was shown that the most horrible and wholesale system
of flogging and branding prevailed throughout the West
Indies. The names, the facts, the places, the dates,
were given. Women actually with child had been
scourged with as many as a hundred and seventy lashes.
Women had been stripped, tied up to a post, and left

there naked through a whole day, writhing under a tropical sun and with a flogging inflicted at stated intervals. Half-caste women, almost as white as English women, were frequently to be identified by the brand on their breasts. The newspapers of the islands constantly contained advertisements for runaway slaves. Nearly all of these were to be identified by the brandings or the marks of flogging. It was occasionally emphasised as a means of identifying a particular woman that she was branded on both breasts. So long before as May 1823, Buxton brought on his first motion for the abolition of slavery. The resolution declared the slavery system repugnant to the principles of the British Constitution and of the Christian religion, and declared that it ought to be gradually abolished throughout the British colonies, with such expedition as may be found consistent with a due regard for the well-being of the parties concerned. Canning was then the leading member of the House of Commons. He did not go so far as to support Buxton, but he proposed three resolutions affirming the expediency of improving the condition of the slaves, preparing them for civil freedom, and at the same time pledging the House to take care that all this should be compatible with the well-being of the slaves, the safety of the colonies, and a full consideration for the rights of private property. These resolutions were adopted, and the colonists urged to take at least one step towards complying with their spirit by abolishing the flogging of women.

The colonies, of course, were under different systems of government. Some were under the direct authority of the Colonial Office, others were governed by local legislatures. Jamaica was one of these, and its House of Assembly was furious with anger at the idea of the British legislature attempting to interfere in the affairs of the colony. In Jamaica there were nearly a half a million of negroes. Barbadoes and Demerara, the latter a crown colony, governed directly by the Colonial Office, broke into still greater fury of wrath. In Demerara some of the slaves had heard vague rumours from England that the day of their freedom was coming, and in a part of the colony they refused to work. Their refusal was called an insurrection, and the insurrection was stamped out with the most savage cruelty. An English missionary, the Rev. John Smith, a dissenter, was charged with inciting the slaves to revolt. He was imprisoned; he was treated with barbarous severity; he was tried with utter disregard of most of the forms of justice, found guilty, and sentenced to death. He escaped the scaffold, however. He died in consequence of the ill-treatment he had suffered, while some of his prosecutors, less cruel than others, were pleading that the recommendation to mercy with which the court-martial had accompanied its verdict ought to be made a reality. The whole question was taken up in England. Brougham, Mackintosh, and Lushington denounced the proceedings of the court-martial. The minister reversed the proceedings of the court, and even when they had made this necessary concession to justice and decency, Brougham's motion, denouncing the whole transaction, was defeated by 193 to 146. The Colonial Office at once issued new regulations for the treatment of slaves in the Crown colonies. These regulations prevented the driver from carrying a whip in the field, abolished altogether the flogging of women, ordered that no punishment should be inflicted until twenty-four hours at least after the offence, that no slave should receive more than twenty-five lashes in one day, and that married slaves were not to be separated from their children. This was

undoubtedly an improvement so far as the Crown colonies
were concerned, but it was not easy to get the local au-
thories of Jamaica to legislate.   In 1826 they did indeed
pass what professed to be an Act to amend the slave
laws, but the Act had nothing really valuable in it.   It
allowed the use of a whip in the field, and it did not
abolish or interfere in any way with the flogging of
women.   The Colonial Office declined to sanction the Act.
The Jamaica Assembly would not assent to the views of
the Colonial Office, and thus the supposed reform dropped
through altogether.   In May 1830, a great meeting was
held in London to agitate again for the total abolition of
slavery, Wilberforce, who had long been out of public
life owing to illness, presiding, and Mr. Buxton proposed
a resolution calling on the country to agitate for the entire abolition of slavery throughout the British dominions.
    One of the results of this meeting was that Lord
Brougham raised the whole question in the House of
Commons.   He brought forward a motion in the close of
the session of 1830, on the general subject of slavery.   He
narrated some of the most appalling stories of the abuse
of despotic power in the colonies.   He thrilled the House
by his eloquence and his passion.   His motion was
defeated, as the motion of an independent member in
such a case is almost sure to be, but the course he had
taken succeeded in arousing the attention of the country,
and making the question of abolition one which no
Government could long afford to neglect.   Mr. Buxton
drew attention to the subject the following year.   Lord
Althorp, unable to accept Buxton's propositions, offered
a poor sort of compromise, the effect of which was that
the colonies which really improved the condition of their
slaves should be allowed to import their sugar into this
country at reduced rates of duty.   This absurd and

feeble suggestion to bribe the planters into a little moderation towards their slaves would have been unworthy of serious consideration, even if the whole question had merely referred to the physical treatment of the unfortunate serfs. But the question, in the mind of Buxton, and now of the country in general, was whether slavery should exist at all, whether it should be abolished unconditionally, or whether, at least, some steps should be taken to insure its gradual extinction. Parliament, however, was dissolved almost immediately after, in consequence of the Reform Bill, and the newly-elected House of Commons was for some time occupied with other subjects. When Parliament met in 1833, everyone expected that the speech from the throne would contain some allusion to the question of emancipation. No word, however, in the speech, long though it was, had any reference to the subject of slavery. Buxton, therefore, at once gave notice of a motion on the question, and appealed to the Government to say whether they did not really intend to introduce a measure themselves. The Government asked for some time to consider the course they could take. In the meantime, Lord Goderich, Secretary of the Colonies, had been transferred to the office of Lord Privy Seal, and the department of the Colonies was placed in charge of Lord Stanley. Lord Stanley was just the man to undertake a bold and hazardous task. He set to work to study the whole question of colonial slavery, and in a few weeks after his acceptance of office, he was enabled to state the policy of the Government on that subject. The speech has been described by all who heard it as a masterpiece of eloquence. The subject was one which exactly harmonised with his impetuous and generous nature. When Lord Stanley's feelings were really roused in some great cause, he was always able to rise to the height of a genuine eloquence. He was not a man of lofty intellect, or even, perhaps, of deeply-penetrating intelligence, but his style, when animated by feeling, carried with it all the persuasiveness and all the force which are especially adapted to move an assembly like the English Parliament. Lord Stanley proposed a plan, the effect of which was that slavery proper should cease at once, but that in order to prepare the slave for the freedom he was ultimately to have, and to meet the chance of the emancipated negroes plunging into excesses of any kind, there should be a transition period—a time of apprenticeship before the negro became a thorough free man. The Colonial Secretary moved five resolutions, one declaring the opinion of the House "that immediate and effectual measures be taken for the entire abolition of slavery throughout the colonies, under such provisions for regulating the condition of the negroes as may combine their welfare with the interests of the proprietors." The second declared it expedient that all children born after the passing of an Act of Parliament for this purpose, or who should be under the age of six years at that time, should be declared free ; " subject, nevertheless, to such temporary restrictions as may be deemed necessary for their support and maintenance." The third declared all persons now slaves entitled to be registered as apprenticed labourers, and to acquire thereby all the rights and privileges of free men, " subject to the restriction of labouring under conditions and for a time to be fixed by Parliament for their present owners." The fourth resolution enabled the Government to advance by way of a loan, to be raised from time to time, a sum not exceeding 15,000,000*l.*, to provide against the risk of loss which proprietors of slaves might sustain by the abolition of slavery. The fifth merely authorised the Crown to meet the expense necessary for establishing a staff of stipendiary magistrates in the colonies, and giving the local magistrates means to provide for the religious and moral education of the emancipated slaves.

The first and second resolutions were adopted after some discussion, but the third resolution, which contained the principles of the apprenticeship system, gave rise to a strong opposition. Mr. Buxton himself led the Opposition, and was followed by the professed friends of emancipation. Lord Howick, son of Earl Grey, also opposed this part of the scheme. He contended that the proposed interval of apprenticeship would in no way improve the character of the negroes, or render them more fit for the enjoyment of perfect liberty at the expiration of twelve years. He had given evidence of his sincerity on the subject by the fact that he resigned the office of Under-Secretary for the Colonies on account of the objection he felt to this part of the Ministerial scheme. Among those who supported the Government was Mr. T. B. Macaulay, afterwards famous as the historian, essayist. and orator. Mr. Macaulay spoke with all the more influence because he was the son of that Zachary Macaulay who had done more than almost any other man for the cause of emancipation, at a period when that cause was yet only beginning its struggles, and seemed to have little chance indeed of approaching success, Macaulay and others contended that the transition from slavery to a state of apprenticeship was, at all events, a great step in advance, that it settled the question of slavery, and that the delay of a few years was a matter of little consequence, as long as absolute emancipation was to follow in its course. Mr. Buxton was prevailed upon to withdraw his amendment and substitute another, to the effect that the labour of the emancipated slaves in the apprenticeship period should be for wages. Further pressure induced him to withdraw this amendment too, but Mr. O'Connell, who had seconded him and who was an uncompromising opponent of slavery in every form, would not give way, pressed the amendment to a division and carried forty votes with him against 324. The resolution which proposed the loan of 15,000,000*l.* to the planters was fiercely opposed by that party in Parliament which represented their interests, and took up their cause. The Government were most unwilling to be defeated in so great a public question, because of a mere difficulty about a sum of money. They therefore agreed to change the proposed loan of 15,000,000*l.* into an absolute gift of 20,000,000*l.* There might have been a good deal said against the policy of an absolute gift. There was certainly enough of what might be called superfluous and unnecessary injustice perpetrated or allowed by the planters as a body, to warrant any Government in refusing absolutely to buy them out of their odious privileges. The Government, however, acted wisely in not haggling about terms, and the country was willing to fling almost any amount of money away in order to get rid of so detestable a system. The resolution, therefore, was carried without a division. It passed the House of Lords along with the rest. A Bill based on all the resolutions was promptly brought in and easily carried with a single change, reducing the term of apprenticeship from twelve years to seven in one class and seven to five in another. Thus the slaves were made free, and the planters were bought out of their privileges. Many of them found themselves positively enriched by the sum of money which fell to their share. They had as a body no part of the credit of the emancipation. They had not even such perverted honour as might fall to the lot of the planters of the Southern States of America, who, believing themselves justified in maintaining their privileges, held both to the last, and preferred war ; for the men of the Southern States could only be forced to yield by superior strength, and were not to be bought or bribed out of their ill-omened claims. The Liverpool merchants were deeply concerned in the slave trade. Cooke, the famous actor, was once hissed in a Liverpool theatre for some offence he had committed. He came forward as if to apologise, and, amid the silence of an expectant audience, hissed out the words : " There is not a stone in the walls of Liverpool but is cemented by the blood of Africans." The saying was a little rude and out of place just then, but it was metaphorically if not literally true.

Another reform of no small importance was accomplished when the charter of the East India Company came to be renewed in 1833. The clause giving them a commercial monoply of the trade of the East was abolished, and the trade thrown open to the merchants of the world.

There were other slaves in those days as well as the negro. There were slaves at home, slaves to all intents and purposes, who were condemned to a servitude as rigorous as that of the negro, and who, as far as personal treatment went, suffered more severely than negroes in the better class plantations. We speak now of the workers in the great mines and factories. No law up to this time regulated with anything like reasonable stringency the hours of labour in factories. Not merely men, but women and children were forced to work for a number of hours absolutely inconsistent with physical health. A commission was appointed to investigate the condition of those who worked in the factories. Lord Ashley, since everywhere known as the Earl of Shaftesbury, was then at the opening of his long career of practical benevolence. Lord Ashley brought forward the motion which ended in the appointment of the commission. The commission quickly brought together an immense amount of evidence to show the terrible effect, moral and physical, of the overworking of women and children, and an agitation set in for the purpose of limiting by law the duration of the hours of labour. This raised a most important economical question. Many men of undoubted humanity and good feeling towards the working classes were strongly opposed to the idea, and maintained not only that it was an improper interference with the operations of private industry on the part of the Government, but that it would end in great injury to the workers themselves. Lord Ashley, however, won the day. The principle of legislative interference to protect children working in factories was established by an Act passed in 1833, limiting the work of children to eight hours a day, and that of young persons under eighteen to sixty-nine hours a week. The agitation then set on foot and led by Lord Ashley was engaged for years after in endeavouring to give that principle a more extended application. A kind of side controversy began between the representatives of the landowning interest and the representatives of the manufacturing interest. Many of the latter earnestly opposed the whole plan of legislation. Its result, they contended, must necessarily be to interfere injuriously with the trade of the country, and thereby to deprive the men of the employment on which they and their families had to live. It would be impossible, they contended, to apply any general rule to all the various branches of manufacturing industry. It would be impossible to find any one law which could work with equal effect on different sorts of business requiring different hours; on business which comes with a rush at one period of the year and is almost slack at another; on business in which much depends on the assisting labour of women and children, and other occupations in which the women and children might be restricted as to their labour without any cessation of the operations of the establishment. Then, seeing that the reform was greatly pressed by benevolent landowners, the manufacturers retorted upon them and asked them what was the condition of their working labourers. The manufacturers insisted that the condition of children employed in agricultural labour called far more loudly for the intervention of the State than that of the children at work in a Lancashire cotton mill. Moreover, the men employed in the mills, they insisted, were well looked after, were well paid, and were therefore very well able to take care not only of themselves but of their wives and children. On the other hand, the wretched labourer of Dorsetshire or Somersetshire never had more than was just enough to keep himself and his children from starvation, and at the end of his weary career of drudgery the workhouse was his only refuge. Why then, they asked, not make laws for him, or if not for him, why not at least protect by legislation his wife and his children from the consequences of overwork?

The controversy was of some interest at the time, but it has little importance for us now. Parliament has long since established the principle that it is part of the right and the duty of the State to look after not merely the labour of children but also the conditions under which adult women are set to work. Parliament since that time has gone on advancing and advancing in the path of such legislation. It will no doubt some day or other undertake to do for the children working in the fields something like that which it has done for the women and children working in the factories. It is now admitted that the legislation for the factories has worked with almost entirely beneficent results. None of the evils anticipated from it have come to pass. Almost all the good it proposed to do has been realised. Each further step of extension in the same direction has been made with satisfactory results.

Lord Ashley obtained at a later period a commission to inquire into the effects of the employment of women and girls in mines. It was found that in some of the coal mines women were employed as beasts of burden in the literal sense. The seams of coal were sometimes too narrow to allow them to stand upright, and they had therefore to crawl back and forwards on their hands and knees for fourteen or sixteen hours a day, drawing after them the trucks laden with coals. These trucks were usually made fast to a chain which passed between the legs of the women engaged in the work, and was then attached to a belt strapped round their waists. The women seldom wore any clothing but an old pair of trousers made of sacking. They were dressed like the men, and only differed from the men in the fact that they had to do the most laborious and degrading part of the work. The physical and moral injuries created by such a state of things need hardly be described. The mind must be dull indeed which has not imagination enough to conceive them. The agitation which Lord Ashley set on foot ended in the passing of an Act of Parliament prohibiting for ever the employment of wo- men or girls underground in the mines. Children were not allowed to be employed at all until they were at least ten years of age, and then their hours for work were limited. Government officials were intrusted with the supervision of the mines in order to see that the enactments were honestly and thoroughly carried out.

It seems almost certain that for some time to come, at least, Parliament will go on enlarging the sphere of its experiments of 1833, in regulating the hours and conditions of labour for the working classes. A strong effort has been recently made to resist the claim of Government to interfere for the protection of the grown women employed in various branches of industry, and it has been made professedly in the interest and on behalf of the free rights of women. But it is only fair to observe that until Parliament makes up its mind to recognize women as citizens entitled to a vote, it is hardly reasonable to seek to withdraw from women the protection which assuredly those have a right to claim who are not allowed to protect themselves. Those who opposed the principle of the factory legislation were, however, in many instances, men of the purest and most unselfish motives, who sincerely believed that any attempt on the part of the Government or the legislature to interfere with the conditions of labour would end not in serving but in seriously injuring the very class whom it was especially proposed to benefit. The course of legislation on the subject of labour seems to have passed through three distinct stages. For generations, and even for centuries, the only legislation which took notice of the condition of the labourer was legislation to coerce him, legislation to put him absolutely at the mercy of his employer. Then there came a short time during which it was maintained that the working of economic principles and of absolute freedom of contract would be enough to undo the evils that centuries of bad legislation

H

and ignorance of social and hygienic laws had engen-
dered. " Leave things to themselves," was the dogma
of that time, " and they will come right." To this period
succeeded the third season, that of energetic desire to
intervene in every possible way and direction for the
regulation of labour in the interest of the working
classes. This last period of activity has certainly not
yet worked itself thoroughly out. The evils which generations of a different sort of principle had created have
not yet been wholly rooted out. When it has fully done
its work, it too, we may be sure, will come to an end.
At present, however, the balance has not yet been properly adjusted, and legislation has still something to do
in the interest of the working man before it can repair
all the injury which it did in the days when it was only
busy to coerce and oppress him.

CHAPTER VIII.

THE IRISH TITHE WAR.

IRISH tithes were one of the grievances which came
under the energetic action of this period of reform.
The people of Ireland complained with justice of having
to pay tithes for the maintenance of the church establishment in which they did not believe, and under
whose roof they never bent in worship. Sydney Smith
had well said of the Irish Church in his own peculiar
fashion : " There is no abuse like it in all Europe, in all
Asia, in all the discovered parts of Africa, and in all we
have ever heard of Timbuctoo." " On an Irish Sabbath,"
he said, " the bell of a neat parish church often summons
to church only the parson and an occasionally conform-
ing clerk, while two hundred yards off a thousand

Catholics are huddled together in a miserable hovel and pelted by all the storms of heaven." To the collection of tithes, he declared, "in all probability about one million of lives may have been sacrificed in Ireland." A miserable, petty civil war was always smouldering; many times the parson's dues had to be collected at the point of the bayonet and with the aid of musket shot. Riots took place. Men were killed on both sides. One of the most thrilling speeches ever made by O'Connell was that in which he describes a fearful scene that took place at a tithe riot, when a blind man was led near the scene of the struggle by a little girl, his daughter. A bullet from one of the police, passing across the field of fight, struck the harmless child and killed her, and the blind father found her blood flowing over his hands. It is stated that Charles Dickens was a reporter in the Gallery at the time when O'Connell made this speech. He was skilled in his craft to an extent which has rarely been equalled, but he threw down his pencil in the middle of the speech, and declared himself so much overpowered by the pathos of the description and of the orator's manner that he was unable to get on with his task. In the county of Kildare a very serious struggle arose, partly out of the tithe question pure and simple, and partly out of a broader religious controversy. There were two over-zealous curates of the Established Church in neighbouring parishes. One anxious to rebuild the parish church succeeded "by packing a vestry with Protestants," as Mr. Walpole puts it in his "History of England," in obtaining a rate for the purpose. The example was followed by the other clergyman. The parishioners, irritated by this, formed an association in which they determined never to pay tithe or church cess in voluntary cash payment again. The unpopularity of the Protestant clergymen of that district greatly increased. An act done by one of them tended to embitter it. The Roman Catholic priest had been usually exempted in Ireland from the payment of the tithe, to which, no doubt, he as well as any other parishioner was legally liable. In one instance, however, a clergyman who was also a magistrate for the county and tithe proctor to the incumbent, an absentee, departed from the usual convenient principle, demanded tithes from the priest, and seized the priest's horse in default of payment. The parish priest of the place denounced from the pulpit the whole system and principle of tithes. Shortly after the cattle of two farmers were seized for tithes, and were released only on a promise that they should be brought up for sale in a fortnight. An impression got abroad among the tithe collectors that the cattle would not be brought up on the appointed day. The clergyman applied for assistance and a strong force police was brought to the place. The principal town of the place was occupied by more than three hundred police, while dragoons and infantry were stationed at adjoining villages. The police were turned, for the time, into cattle drivers ; perhaps it should rather be said that they were turned for the time into a foraging party engaged in futile attempts to get cattle in order to drive them off. Wherever the police were supposed to be coming the cattle were locked up, and it was not legal to break open a lock in order to get at them. The efforts of the police were therefore, in most instances, reduced to nothing. .In some few exceptional cases where the police did succeed in capturing some of the cattle, no bidder could be found for them at the sale except the owner himself. They had therefore to be sold for a merely nominal price. A tithe collection which had to be conducted on this principle naturally brought but little profit to the Church authorities. The same kind of dexterity and perseverance was shown in evading the collection of tithes which in later days has been shown in evading the levy of distress warrants for the collection of arrears of rent. It required the marching and counter marching of fatigue parties, *reconnaissances*, sorties, military expeditions of various kinds, and a regular army of police and soldiers to secure to a country clergyman the tithes which he claimed of a reluctant and hostile parish.

The resistance, thus brought into organised shape, was not slow in spreading over parishes and counties. It was not then lawful to hold a public meeting in Ireland, but no law prevented people from gathering together for an Irish sport called a hurling match. Great meetings were brought together in this way. There was an appointment for a hurling match. People came frequently armed, and made no scruple about admitting that their object was not to see who could send the ball farthest along the road, or across the fields, but who could lend the most efficient assistance in driving the tithe system out of the country. Intimidation was exercised by these crowds upon mild parishioners who were willing to pay the tithe which they detested for the sake of living at quiet with their neighbours. They were taught to feel that if they could by this process conciliate the Protestant clergy, and relieve themselves from interference by the police, they only brought down on their shoulders the much more formidable oppression of their fellow-religionists and fellow-parishioners. Resistance to the payment of tithes very soon grew into organised resistance to the payment of rent. When men were made prisoners for nearly any offence of this kind it was found practically impossible to obtain a conviction.

Lord Grey announced on one occasion that the Government were determined to enforce the law while it existed,
but enforcement of the law in any practical sense was
now out of the question. With great good fortune and
almost supernatural courage and energy the Government
might possibly have succeeded in punishing any very
daring and exceptional offender against the public peace,
but the idea of securing the collection of tithes by any
administrative energy or ability was no longer to be
entertained by any rational creature. Armies could not
have collected the tithes, and the very efforts to collect
them only brought increased and increasing hardship
and distress on the poorer of the Protestant clergy themselves. Active resistance may be easily put down, even
by a weak Government, but a determined and organised
passive resistance, suppressed here and there, but always reforming itself on opportunity and having the sympathy of the great mass of the community, is beyond the
reach of any administrative power.

Many of the Protestant clergymen themselves were beginning to find their positions untenable, and to lament the
unavailing bloodshed which attended the effort to collect
the obnoxious tithes. Their own interests were gradually
bringing them to join with their opponents in desiring an
abolition of the system. A committee of the House of
Lords reported that a complete extinction of tithes was
required, not only for the welfare of Ireland but for the
interests of the Church itself, and added that this extinction might be obtained " by commuting them for a charge
upon land," or by " an exchange for an investment in
land." A committee of the House of Commons made a
report in which they declared themselves unable to shut
their eyes to the absolute necessity of an extensive change
in the present system of providing for the ministers of

the Established Church. They gave it as their opinion
that such a change, to be satisfactory and secure, " must
involve a complete extinction of tithes, including those of
lay impropriators, by commuting them for a charge upon
land." These reports, therefore, from the two Houses of
Parliament, were produced in 1832. They practically
agreed in purpose, and each of them suggested a temporary measure for the relief of the interests now suffering
under the struggle. They recommended that the Government should be authorised to advance to every incumbent a sum not exceeding the amount due to him as tithes
for 1831, and that the Government should then be authorised to buy up the arrears of tithes and to repay
itself for its advances out of the sum which they might
recover.

On March 8, 1832, the Government announced their
intention to take steps to give effect to the object of these
reports. It was also announced that the Government
desired to supplement their measure for the temporary
collection of tithes by some Bill which would result in
their absolute extinction, either by commuting them for
a charge on land or exchanging them for real property.
The House of Lords accepted the measure easily enough,
with no resistance greater than was contained in a protest from Lord Eldon. The House of Commons were
not equally willing to accept the scheme. On the part
of the Irish members it was insisted that the only change
was to turn the Government into a tithe collector, and
that the existence of tithes, not the mode of their collection, was the grievance of which Ireland complained.
The Government, however, succeeded in carrying three
resolutions, affirming that a difficulty had arisen, that it
would be expedient for the time to distribute a sum of
money among distressed incumbents, and authorising the

Government to collect the tithes the best way they could, in order to recover these advances. Having obtained the carrying of these resolutions, they went a little further by adding two resolutions which pledged the Legislature to deal with the tithe system as a whole at the earliest opportunity. The Bill, when thus made complete, was opposed in various ways in both Houses, but it carried substantial majorities at each reading and at each stage, and finally passed into law.

Year after year the Government kept tinkering at the tithe system. They tried various plans of composition for tithes, now leaving the task of collection to the landlord who compounded, and now accepting it as the business of the State and making grants of money to supply deficiencies. O'Connell once said the Government had made the Lord-Lieutenant tithe-proctor-general for Ireland. But the viceregal tithe-proctor could not get in his tithes any more than the parson's tithe-proctor had done. In 1833 the arrears of tithes amounted to nearly a million and a quarter of money. The Government prevailed on the House of Commons to advance a million to be handed over to the tithe owners on the security of the arrears, and the House saw the water poured into the sieve. The tithe question was but a part of the Church question in Ireland. That general question was brought up in 1834 by Mr. Ward, one of the most rising among the new members of the House of Commons. He was a son of that Plumer Ward, author of a popular novel once called "Tremaine," which now lives in the memory of novel readers less by virtue of its own merits than by the fact that it is referred to in Lord Beaconsfield's "Vivian Grey." Henry Ward won some distinction afterwards as an administrator in the Ionian Islands and in Ceylon. Mr. Walpole, in his "His-

tory of England," says that Ward is remembered by
a few persons "for the witty epigram which praises his
memory at the expense of his affections." The epigram
is:

> Ward has no heart, they say, but I deny it;
> He has a heart, and gets his speeches by it.

These lines, however, we think, were not written for
Henry Ward. They were written by Rogers and referred to John W. Ward, afterwards Lord Dudley and
Ward. Henry Ward, however, was at this time a rising
politician, and had formed very ·strong opinions with
regard to the condition and the revenues of the Irish
Church. He was convinced that the revenues were much
more than sufficient for the requirements of the Establishment, and that any surplus not needed for the Church
ought to be appropriated by Parliament to other and
more public purposes. He brought‵forward a resolution
setting forth this opinion. The debate on the resolution
was fixed for May 27, 1834, and it formed an era in the
history of the Irish Church Establishment.

Many persons, among whom Lord Palmerston was
one, were of opinion that Mr. Ward, in bringing forward
his motion, was acting merely on the inspiration of Lord
Durham. It is not at all unlikely that Lord Durham
may have suggested the course which at that time seemed
so bold.

Mr. Ward's motion declared "that the Protestant
Episcopal Establishment in Ireland exceeds the spiritual
wants of the Protestant population, and that it being the
right of the State to regulate the distribution of Church
property in such manner as Parliament may determine,
it is the opinion of this House that the temporal possessions of the Church of Ireland as now established

ought to be reduced." This would seem to us now to be
so plain a statement of fact as hardly to call for any
argument. But at that time it was regarded as the introduction of a new and daring principle. The arguments with which Mr. Ward sustained his proposition
went in their tendency far beyond the limits of the resolution which he moved. The purpose of the resolution
really was to lay down the principle that the State had a
right to consider the existence of the Irish Church as dependent upon its practical uses for the Irish people. Mr.
Ward went on to show that the tithe collection was the
principal cause of the disturbance and tumult that had
lately been spreading over Ireland. He proved that the
objection and resistance to the payment of tithes was not
now any longer confined to the Catholics only. It had
spread from Catholics to Protestants, from one part of
the country to all parts. The arrangement in existence
at that time and established by Government compromise
would end with the close of the autumn, and then either
the Church must fall back to its old rough system of
tithe collection or be maintained out of the civil funds of
the State. The tithe-collectors had tried civil law and
military force, and in vain. Mr. Ward mentioned the
astonishing fact that for a period of about eight years
there had been maintained in Ireland an army almost
exactly as strong as that which was required for the
government of our whole Indian Empire. It fell short
only by one-third of the military strength which was
needed to occupy all our colonies in the rest of the
world besides. From 1825 to 1833 the military force
had been little below 20,000 at its lowest and about
23,000 at its highest. During the year preceding Mr.
Ward's motion this military force had cost more than a
million of money. The cost of the police force was

about 300,000*l.* in addition. The Government had spent 26,000*l.* in collecting 12,000*l.* of tithes. Mr. Ward also pointed out one great abuse of the Irish Church system, which consisted in the grossly unfair distribution of its revenues, the immense sums paid to clergymen who had nothing to do, and the exceedingly small and miserable stipends doled out to some of the clergy who did whatever work there was to be done. There were nearly as many clergy non-resident as resident. Some of the non-resident clergy had benefices varying in value from 800*l.* to 2,800*l.* a year. Some of the resident clergy, who did the work, had in certain cases incomes as low as 20*l.* a year. An income of 70*l.* was above the average. What kind of respect, Mr. Ward asked, can the Irish people have for such an institution, when they see its actual work done for a miserably small sum, and the great bulk of its revenue given away to men who do nothing? How, he asked, is it possible to suppose that the existence of such an institution, worked in such a way, could attract the Irish Catholics towards it and make them feel inclined to seek comfort in its ministrations? He showed that rather less than one-fourteenth of the whole population of Ireland belonged to the State Church. Indeed, he brought together such a monstrous array of anomalies and abuses as probably could not have been found in the contemporary history of any other civilized country. Mr. Ward recommended a redistribution of the Church revenues in some way which might proportion the pay to the work, and give the pay to the men who did the work. With regard to the tithe system, he was for its entire abolition, because, as he showed, the grievance was not one which could be remedied by any improvement in the manner of collecting the tax. The objection was deep and essential, and consisted in the fact that the great majority who paid the tax for the support of the Church were Catholics, who did not acknowledge its supremacy and who could never be induced to cross the threshold of any of its temples. Mr. Ward made it clear that the maintenance of the Church, such as it was, cost the Government a sum of money far beyond the value of the revenues attached to the Church, large as they were, and that even as a matter of economy it would be cheaper to pay the Irish clergy out of the public funds than to allow the existing system to continue any longer.

The motion was seconded by Mr. Grote, the historian of Greece. Even at this comparatively early day the best independent intellect of the House of Commons was already engaged in an effort to draw the attention of the country to the vast fundamental difference between the conditions of the State Church in Ireland, and those of the State Church in England. Mr. Grote's speech was a remarkable contribution to a memorable debate. He addressed himself chiefly to the task of showing how wide was the difference between the principles on which the two State Churches rested. His speech was in fact a clear and just argument to show that not only were the principles different but that they were fundamentally antagonistic. Those, he said, who compared the two churches would only degrade the one without elevating the other. They were not only not the same, but they were actually opposed in spirit and in principle. One church, as he showed, rested its claim to be national on the plain broad fact that it represented the religious convictions of the great majority of the people. More than this it was, from its representative position, in this respect the natural and the only guardian of what we may call the waifs and strays of the population. If a parentless child were found in the streets or were brought to one of the public institutions, nothing could be more reasonable, nothing in fact could be more necessary, than that it should be supposed to belong to the Church which expressed the religious feelings of the great bulk of the English people. On the other hand the State Church in Ireland represented at the very most the religious opinions of one-fourteenth of the population, and both Mr. Ward and Mr. Grote gave it as their opinion that one-fourteenth was too large a proportion for the members of the Episcopalian Church when compared with the Roman Catholics and the Dissenters of Ireland. Mr. Grote's speech, though very short, was very effective, and must, one would think, have made some impression on the political intelligence of the time.

It was known already to everyone that Mr. Ward's motion was certain to lead to distraction and to division in the Cabinet itself. Lord Brougham had been endeavouring to establish a compromise by suggesting that a commission should be appointed to inquire into the revenues of the Irish Church, and the proportion which her revenues bore to the whole population of Ireland. It is clear that this was a suggestion which opponents of disestablishment could not possibly accept. A man like Lord Stanley, for instance, whose principle it was that the Irish Church must be maintained, both as a piece of mechanism for the sustentation of English power and as a possible agency towards the ultimate conversion of the Irish people to Protestantism, could not possibly admit that the future fate of the Church should depend upon the proportion of worshippers which entered the doors of its temples. Once start such a principle as this, and the result, however long postponed, was certain to follow.

Once admit that the State had the right to dispose of the revenues of the Irish Church itself with any regard for the opinions and professions of the majority of the Irish public, and there could be no issue but one; the Church State Establishment must fall. Lord Stanley, therefore, set himself against any compromise and any commission such as Brougham proposed. Mr. Ward's introduction of his motion led at once to the resignation of Lord Stanley the Colonial Secretary, Sir James Graham First Lord of the Admiralty, Lord Ripon Privy Seal, and the Duke of Richmond Postmaster-General. On the very night when Mr. Ward brought forward his motion Lord Althorp learnt that his colleagues had resigned, and rose to ask the House for the adjournment of the debate.

It was after Mr. Grote's speech that Lord Althorp thus appealed to the House of Commons to consent to an adjournment, because, as he said, of facts which had come to his knowledge since the debate began. He frankly acknowledged that it was not in his power at present to state the exact nature of the facts, but he appealed to the House to accept his assurance, that he would not have made such a proposition without having been satisfied of its propriety and its necessity. Everyone knew at once that the Ministerial crisis had come. Everyone knew also what its cause and its nature must have been, and most people were able even to tell in advance the names of the men on both sides who were concerned in the undoubted disruption of the Ministry. Before the crisis was complete some of the independent or semi-independent friends of the Ministry hastened to get up an address to Lord Grey, imploring him, whatever might happen, to remain at the head of the Government, and declaring that the confidence of the House of

Commons and of the country was still entirely given to him. Lord Grey, in replying to the address, declared that he was prepared to make every personal sacrifice in support of the principles for which he had taken office, but he complained in his clear, cold, and somewhat sharp manner, of the harm that was being done to the progress of Liberal principles by the heedless desire for innovation. He declared that to him it seemed indispensable, if any improvement was to be made in the institutions of the country, that the Government should be allowed to go on with deliberation and with caution, and that they should not be harassed by a constant pressure from without to go further and faster than seemed necessary to them. Lord Grey's reply made it more clear than almost anything else had done that a crisis had arisen in the history, not merely of the Whig Cabinet but of the Liberal party. It was evident that the time had now come when a certain number of the Whigs were disinclined to go any further. The Liberal party was now distinctly dividing itself into Whigs and Radicals. On the other hand some who up to that moment were Whigs were now clearly about to fall away and join the Conservative ranks. The impulse and the energy of the reform movement had welded together for a certain time three strands of the party, the Conservative portion, the Whig portion, the Radical portion. The strands were now about to separate.

The adjournment of the debate took place as a matter of course. There was nothing to be done but to adjourn and give the Government time to reorganize itself The discussion was resumed with the reconstitution of the Ministry. Lord Conyngham had become Postmaster-General in place of the Duke of Richmond. Lord Auckland had taken Sir James Graham's position at the head of the Admiralty, Lord Carlisle became Privy Seal, and Mr. Spring-Rice, afterwards Lord Monteagle, who had been for some years Secretary of the Treasury, succeeded Lord Stanley in the Colonial Office. When the debate was renewed Lord Althorp rose and announced to Mr. Ward that the Government had made up their minds to issue a commission to inquire into the whole question as to the revenues and organisation of the Irish Church, and he appealed to Mr. Ward to withdraw his motion in favour of this proposal, urging that there would have to be an inquiry by commission or otherwise before legislation could take place even if Mr. Ward's motion were carried, and therefore it would be as well to save the trouble of a debate and a division, and issue a commission at once. To this Mr. Ward made a very reasonable answer. He admitted that the commission would have to be issued, but if his resolution were carried the commission would be issued under very different auspices from those which would surround it if it were to be issued before the adoption of his motion. His resolution, if carried, would pledge the House of Commons to the principle that the revenues of the State Church in Ireland were absolutely under the control of Parliament. That principle, it is true, the present Ministry fully acknowledged, and therefore a commission issued by them would no doubt be animated by the recognition of such a fact. But they might go out of office at any moment. Facts occurring every day showed that their tenure of power was not particularly secure, nor their continued coherence much to be depended on. Their successors, therefore, would be by no means pledged to any such principle, or to any course of action to follow a report from the commission. On the other hand a distinct and deliberate vote of the House of Commons would undoubtedly, Mr. Ward contended, have some influence over the action of any subsequent Ministry, however illiberal and reactionary. He therefore firmly refused to withdraw his motion. Lord Althorp then said he had no course left but to evade the difficulty by moving the previous question.

Perhaps it may be an advantage to some of our readers unskilled in the formalities of the House of Commons, to explain what is meant by moving the previous question. A motion for some particular purpose is before the House of Commons. That motion is what is called a question. The Government are not disinclined to admit the principle contained in the motion, but they have some reason for thinking the present time unsuited for such a debate. They are unable to vote for the motion because they think its discussion inconvenient and perhaps dangerous just then. They do not feel inclined to vote directly against it, because that might imply that they are opposed to its general principle, which they are not. It is therefore open to them to get out of the difficulty by moving "the previous question," as it is called; that is, by raising the question whether the motion ought to be put. They move, in substance, as an amendment that this is not the proper time for discussing the question, and that the motion before the chair be not put to a division. Lord Althorp voted in this instance that Mr. Ward's motion be not put to a division. The debate which followed was animated, and is interesting to read even now. On the part of the Government the only case urged against Mr. Ward's motion was that which we have already suggested, that the Government were about to issue a commission, that inquiry must follow in any case, and therefore the adoption of the motion was a mere waste of power and loss of time. On the other

I

hand, Lord Stanley and Sir Robert Peel strongly opposed the motion on direct and simple grounds. Lord Stanley contended, and justly, that the adoption of such a motion associated the existence of the Irish State Church in principle with the proportion of representation which it had in the community. He contended, and justly, that by admitting Mr. Ward's motion Parliament claimed for itself the right to abolish a State Church in Ireland altogether, if the proportion of its worshippers were greatly below that of the rest of the community. He contended that, according to the principle of a State Church, it did not matter how few were the worshippers: he urged, indeed, that the fewer there were, the more necessity there was for such an institution. What, he asked, is there in our Parliamentary system which, if this resolution were passed, would not leave the Government open to establish a Roman Catholic Church in Ireland if they thought fit? Of course the answer to this is plain. As long as the Imperial Government recognises the Protestant as the State religion, it is certain that it will not establish a Roman Catholic Church in Ireland. On the other hand it is equally certain that if the majority of the English people were Roman Catholics, and were inclined to maintain a State Church, they would establish a Catholic Church. We cannot have the same State Church resting on the principle of a majority in England and on the principle of a minority in Ireland. But Lord Stanley was right in saying that the moment we recognise the supremacy of numbers at all we foredoom an institution like the State Church in Ireland. Sir Robert Peel dwelt strongly on that feeblest of all arguments (so feeble that it seems at this distance of time a marvel to find it put forward by so great a statesman), the argument that the Catholics had pledged themselves at the time of their emancipation, from the lips of Grattan, and even in the preambles of Acts of Parliament, not to ask for any measure which could affect the Established Church in Ireland. It seems marvellous how such a man could have relied on such an argument, or could have assumed that it was in the power of one generation of men to bind their successors to a surrender of any fair and legitimate claims. Of course when a generation of men are seeking some right which they greatly desire to have, they are ready enough to undertake that if they get this they will ask for no more. The mere fact that such a promise is made is more discreditable to those who accept than to those who make it. It can hardly be serious in the mouths of those who make it or in the minds of those who receive it. The argument had been torn to pieces by Sydney Smith and by other authors, even before Sir Robert Peel put it forward thus gravely again. O'Connell spoke in the debate, and spoke with robust good sense as well as with eloquence. He especially cautioned the Government against refusing justice to the Irish people and so driving them into despair, and into that conspiracy which he truly said was the natural offspring of despair. The House divided after a long debate on the issue that the question be now put. One hundred and twenty members voted in favour of putting Mr. Ward's resolution to the vote and 369 against it. A majority of 276 declared, therefore, that the motion was not to be put.

The House hastened to adopt the suggestion of the Government for the issue of a commission. A puzzled Government always falls back on the appointment of a commission. Lord Stanley tried in vain to oppose this compromise, and to show that even the appointment of a commission involved a principle destructive of the very existence of the Established Church. He found little support for this extreme view among the more sensible members of the Tory party. Sir Robert Peel himself was quite willing to consider the propriety and feasibility of redistributing the property of the Church. So far did Peel go in this direction, that it was sneeringly suggested that he ought to have succeeded to the place in the Whig Government vacated by Lord Stanley. As a matter of expediency and of compromise, Sir Robert Peel was undoubtedly right ; but, on the other hand, the view of Lord Stanley was sound and prophetic as regards the fate of the Established Church in Ireland. It is not true that the appointment of a commission involved a principle destructive of the very existence of an Established Church, that is of any Established Church. The right of the State to redistribute the revenues and reorganise the system of an Established Church in a country whose religious opinions it fairly and fully represented would by no means involve any principle fatal to its existence. But in a country where five out of every six of the people were resolutely opposed to the teachings of the State Church, and could never, under any conditions, be brought to cross the threshold of one of its Church buildings, the moment inquiry set in as to the appropriation of its revenues and the right of the State to redistribute them, then indeed, as Lord Stanley contended, the principle was admitted which must inevitably lead to its destruction. Thirty-five years later the principle which the House of Commons adopted when they accepted the compromise suggested by Lord Brougham, was pushed to its legitimate conclusion in the famous suspensory resolutions introduced by Mr. Gladstone when in opposition, and the schemes for the disestablishment and disendowment of the Irish Church which he carried through when in office.

There was fresh effort at tithe compromises, and the Government got into trouble about the renewal of an Irish Coercion Act. Tired of political life, glad of any excuse to escape from it, Lord Grey resigned office, and the Ministry was reorganised, with Lord Melbourne for its leader. Few things are more curious than the contrast between Lord Melbourne's political character and the general character of his administrative work. Lord Melbourne cared little or nothing for reform. He was not interested in change of any kind. He was a genial, easy-going, not incapable, man. The whole principle of his public life might well enough be illustrated in his own favourite remonstrance with energetic reformers and innovators, " Can't you let it alone ?" He would gladly, if he could, have let every proposed change alone. Things seemed to be very well as they were. In any case he was not afforded, just now, much chance of undertaking important work. The King had gradually been turning more and more against his Whig Ministers, because of what he considered their lack of firmness on Church questions. In reply to an address delivered to him on his birthday by a deputation of the Irish prelates, the King made a speech filled with the most earnest protestations of his determination to maintain the Church ; a speech which was in fact a spoken censure on his Ministry. No one was surprised, therefore, when on the occasion of a slight reconstruction of the administration, consequent on the death of Lord Althorp's father, which raised Lord Althorp to the House of Lords, the King bluntly informed Lord Melbourne that he did not intend to go on with his present Ministers any longer. Sir Robert Peel was summoned from Rome to form an administration. Sir Robert Peel undertook the task, but thought it necessary to dissolve Parliament and appeal to

the country. The result of the general election brought
little comfort to the Tories. The Whigs lost much of
their overwhelming power, but they still remained strong
enough to command a majority against the Government
on any convenient occasion. Peel saw a trying task
before him. Few tasks can be more painful and humiliating to a high-spirited statesman than to have to try to
govern with a minority, knowing that there is a sure
majority ready at any moment to declare against him.

The new Parliament met on February 19, 1835. The
opposing parties had a trial of strength in the election of
a Speaker. The Government was defeated by ten
votes; 316 voted one way and 306 the other. Sir Robert
Peel, however, was resolved that he would not resign his
office, but struggle on as best he could. He was again
defeated on the moving of the Address, an amendment
being carried by a majority of seven. Still he did not
think he was called upon to resign, considering the difficulties by which the Government of every kind was em-
barrassed just then. He resolved to do the best he could
to carry on the administration. On March 30, Lord John
Russell moved a resolution calling on the House to
form itself into a committee to consider the state of the
Church Establishment in Ireland, with the view of applying any surplus of the revenues not required for the
spiritual care of its members to the education of all
classes of the people, without distinction of religious denomination. Sir Robert Peel of course strongly opposed
the motion, and he was supported by Lord Stanley and
Sir James Graham. Mr. O'Connell spoke strongly for
the motion. "I shall content myself," he said, "by
laying down the broad principle that the revenues of the
Church ought not to be raised from a people who do not
belong to it." The result of a long debate was another

defeat of the Government; 322 voted for the motion, and 289 against it. A new discussion on the question of Irish tithes exposed the Ministers to yet another defeat. Sir Robert Peel found it impossible to continue in office any longer. He resigned on April 8. An effort was made to induce Lord Grey to form an administration, but Lord Grey was not to be tempted, and the King was at last obliged to send for Lord Melbourne. A few days later an administration was formed, Lord Melbourne for First Lord of the Treasury, Lord Lansdowne President of the Council, Lord Palmerston Foreign Secretary, Lord John Russell Home Secretary, and Mr. Spring-Rice Chancellor of the Exchequer.

Among other members of the new Government may be mentioned Sir Henry Parnell, whose motion not long before had upset the Government of the Duke of Wellington. Sir J. C. Hobhouse, the friend of Byron, took charge of the India Department. Lord Morpeth became Chief Secretary of the Lord Lieutenant of Ireland.

The new Government had come into power by defeating their predecessors on the subject of the Irish Church and Irish tithes, and, of course, they had to undertake some sort of legislation in harmony with the professions and the policy which they relied upon when in opposition. Accordingly, on June 26, 1835, Lord Morpeth introduced a Tithe Bill. Lord Morpeth was the eldest son of Lord Carlisle. He was well known in later days as one of the most pleasing and popular Viceroys Ireland ever had. He was a man of a certain graceful literary style, both in writing and in speaking, of agreeable, kindly manners, and winning social ways. He might have been a successful Viceroy if his lot had been cast in times when genial good manners and graceful accomplishments were sufficient stock-in-trade for a

Lord Lieutenant of Ireland. At the time, however, to which we now refer, he was practically an untried statesman learning his business in the Irish Office. His Tithes Bill was a distinct advance on anything which his predecessors had introduced. Twelve years before, Mr. Goulburn had introduced the principle of the voluntary composition of tithes. Nine years later Mr. Stanley had made composition compulsory. In 1834 Mr. Littleton endeavoured to convert the composition into a rent charge. In 1835 the Government proposed to convert the tithe itself into a rent charge. All parties, therefore, had come to an agreement that the tithe as a burden should be transferred from the occupier to the owner, and all too were willing that the rent charge should be much smaller than the tithe, and that the titheowner should sacrifice some portion of his income in return for the better security he was to have. Lord Morpeth proposed to reduce the rent charge to a lower amount than any of his predecessors. He proposed to commute one hundred pounds of tithe for seventy pounds of rent charge. He proposed to charge on the owner of the tithes the cost of collection, and to abandon to the owner the uncollected arrears of tithes on the security of which the Government had made liberal advances of money. But his measure did not stop with the simple adjustment of tithes. He proposed to act on the spirit of Lord John Russell's resolution, and introduce certain appropriation clauses, as they were called, to deal with the surplus revenues of the Irish Church. No presentation was to be made for the time to any benefice which did not contain at least fifty members of the Church of England. But in order to provide meanwhile for the religious accommodation of the members of that Church, it was proposed that in parishes where there was no church the minister of the adjoining parish was to receive an additional 5*l.* a year for the cure of souls which might be supposed to exist in the neighbouring district. This Bill was read a first time on July 7. Sir Robert Peel then at once announced that he approved of that part of the Bill which proposed to substitute a rent charge for tithes, but to the clauses which would appropriate to other purposes the property of the Church he was prepared to offer the strongest opposition. He allowed the Bill to be read a second time, but he announced his intention to move in committee that it be divided into two parts, so that those who agreed with him in thinking the existing tithe system ought to be abolished would be free to support that part of the measure without assenting to the other part of it, which dealt with the revenues and arrangements of the Church. When the House went into committee, Sir Robert Peel's amendment to divide the Bill into two was rejected by a majority of 319 against 282. This majority was not large enough to bear down the opposition of the Lords, and accordingly, when the Bill reached the Upper House the Peers adopted the advice which Sir Robert Peel had given to the Commons. They passed that part of the Bill which substituted a rent charge for tithes, and by an enormous majority they struck out the part which dealt with the revenue of the Church. Lord Morpeth's attempt therefore had come to nothing. The Bill was withdrawn.

The same difficulty followed the proposed reform through successive years. The Conservatives persistently refused to agree to any Bill which dealt with any part of the revenues of the State Church. On the other hand, the Government were pledged deeply and again and again to pass no Bill which did not contain an appropriation clause. In 1836 Lord Morpeth brought on his measure again, but the appropriation clause was only carried by 290 votes against 264. Naturally this gave the Peers fresh encouragement. Once again they mutilated the Bill. The Commons refused to accept the amendments, and the Tithe Bill was a failure once more. In 1838 Lord John Russell took up the subject. He introduced a Bill based on the principle which his predecessors had adopted. He proposed to convert the tithe composition into a rent charge of seventy per cent. of the nominal value of the tithe, and to secure this income to existing incumbents by the guarantee of the State. Despite a sort of promise given by Sir Robert Peel that the conservatives would not oppose the measure if it did not contain a sweeping appropriation clause, there was a strong opposition made to it by the Tories. Finally, Lord John Russell consented so far to modify his proposal as to confine the measure merely to a Bill converting the tithe composition into a rent charge. He also went so far as to fix the rent charge at seventy-five per cent. instead of seventy, as he had at first proposed. They introduced clauses giving up the claim of the country to have the great advance already made to the titheowners repaid to the nation, and they agreed to devote a quarter of a million of money to the extinction of the remaining arrears. The more advanced party amongst the English Liberals were enraged at what they called a surrender of principle. They declared that the very object to maintain which Sir Robert Peel had been driven out of office had now been given up by the Whig administration. They insisted that Lord John Russell's Bill simply squandered immense sums of the national money on the Church of a minority. It is plain, indeed, that the Bill which was now passed was in substance the very measure which might have been obtained with the assent of Sir Robert Peel in 1835. The difficulty during many years had been that which we have already described, the question of appropriation—that is, of sequestration of part of the revenues of the State Church and interference with its internal arrangements. To secure that principle the Whigs had stood out against the Tories ; to prevent that principle from being adopted in legislation was for many years the sole object of the Tories. Both parties were willing to agree on the change of the tithe into a rent charge, and the Bill therefore which Lord John Russell passed in 1838 might have been passed many years sooner if the Whig Ministry could have made up their minds as to the distance they were willing to go in order to meet a compromise. Meanwhile the agitation on Irish tithes had produced an agitation about English tithes as well. Many grievances existed in England as well as in Ireland, although,, of course, they were not aggravated in England by the continued and inevitable hostility between the State Church and the people. At the worst, in England, the tithe was unfairly levied and badly appropriated, but in Ireland it was like a humiliating tribute exacted by the conqueror from the conquered. The question was settled in England before its settlement in Ireland. A Bill introduced in 1836 by Lord John Russell made the commutation of tithes compulsory, appointed commissioners to value the tithes on an average estimate of three crops during the seven preceding years, and awarded to the titheowner a commutation not less than sixty per cent. and not more than seventy-five per cent. of the nominal gross value of the tithe. This measure was passed with no practical modification. The commissioners soon succeeded in getting at a rate of commutation for every parish, and the payment of tithe in kind came to an end

in this country. The effect of the measure thus introduced was found in the end to be as satisfactory to the
Church as it was to the tithe payers. The Church obtained a certain revenue in return for the very uncertain
and haphazard kind of collection. The owners and
occupiers found themselves rid of a very disagreeable
and fluctuating kind of charge, the collection of which
was troublesome, and the effect of which was very often
to make the clergyman of the parish an object of dis-
trust and dislike much more than of affection and confidence to his parishioners. But in Ireland the change
in the system of tithe collecting was only a small part of
a great, a necessary, and an inevitable reform, which,
although seen by many even then to be inevitable, was
postponed and resisted for more than a generation.

CHAPTER IX.

POOR LAW AND MUNICIPAL REFORM.

MUCH of the misery of the rural labourer in England
was to be traced directly to the condition of the poor law
system. The famous statute of Elizabeth, which was
intended to put a stop to vagrancy and mendicancy and
to encourage industry, had been worked for generations
in such a manner as to foster pauperism and create quite
a disease of beggary. The laws of settlement, which
were intended merely to protect districts from actual
invasions of hordes of paupers, had practically put it in
the power of parishes which were rich to turn over the
surplus of their labouring population on smaller and
poorer places. When the Reformed Parliament came
into existence, Lord Grey and his colleagues determined

to seek out some cure for the evils which were constantly increasing. They did what was invariably done
by the Whig administrations of that time. They began
by issuing a commission. That was a time when
Sydney Smith said that the whole earth was put into
commission by the Whigs. In this instance the commission was a very important matter, and was composed
of men well qualified for the investigation. The commission appointed assistant commissioners to make the
actual inquiries. The result of the investigation was to
show that the poor law system was administered almost
everywhere in such a manner as to engender abuses
even where abuses had not previously existed. In many
places the local tradesmen and the parish officers played
into each other's hands, as the servants and the tradesmen of a nobleman might be supposed to do. The
tradesmen overcharged for every article they supplied to
the parochial authorities, and the parish officers were
bribed to assist them in this system of extortion. The
poor rates were openly made use of for the purpose of
bribing the holders of the franchise. But probably worse
than all this was the manner in which the system encouraged and promoted pauperism. The pauper in the
workhouse was well fed, and too well fed, at the expense
of the poor ratepayer, who, sometimes but one degree
above the level of pauperism, was too independent to eat
the bread of beggary while he could maintain himself
and his family by any amount of incessant and hopeless
labour. . When a person had once taken poor-house
relief it became a sort of property or inheritance. Once
in the family it never got out of the family. Generations
of paupers bequeathed to the country new generations of
paupers. The character of a recipient was not held to
be any reason for denying relief. He might be a well-

known thief. She might be a well-known prostitute. In either case the relief was given just when it was asked for. A father spent all his wages in drink, and came to get relief for his family when there was nothing to give them at home. In some places whole populations were turned into paupers. People lived on the relief given by the workhouse rather than on wages. Workhouse support was constantly given in relief of wages. A farmer dismissed his labourers because he did not care to pay them the market price of labour; they at once became paupers; they received a certain contribution from the parish and then the farmer took them back and gave them employment at lower wages than before, so that in point of fact the local taxation became a sort of rate in aid of the farmers. In some places the manufacturers followed the example of the farmers, discharged their workpeople, and allowed them to become paupers in the receipt of parish relief, well knowing that when once they had begun to receive that relief no workhouse official would ever challenge their right to the continuance of the dole. They then re-employed them at much lower rates, and so received a subsidy from the parochial funds in aid of their business. It has been distinctly stated that the commissioners found many cases in which men spent their wages as rapidly as they could, in drink or in amusement, in order that they might be able to say they had actually nothing and so be entitled to get their names on the workhouse list. In fact, to have one's name put down as a recipient of workhouse relief was like having it put down on a pension list. Once put down it was not supposed that it would be taken off again unless at the request of the recipient himself. The relieving-officer's book was to the low class ne'er-do-well what the pension list was to his aristocratic fellow. It seems almost needless to say that such a system encouraged early improvidence and reckless marriages. A man might as well marry as not, for he received relief, his wife would receive relief, and as his children began to grow up they would come in for their share of the general subsidy. The evil had grown so great that some eminent reformers were positively of opinion that the only remedy would be the entire abolition of the poor laws, leaving the relief of genuine pauperism to the operation of private benevolence, energy, and supervision.

The commissioners, however, were not of opinion that so sweeping a remedy could be attempted. They held that the principle of public relief was that a certain provision should be made for that surplus, or residuum as it may be called, of every population, the infirm and the aged who have no friends to support them ; for those who, under some temporary pressure, cannot obtain work, however willing to take it; and likewise, it may be added, for those who even by their idleness or misconduct had brought themselves into such a condition, that if not fed for a time at the public expense, they needs must commit actual crime or else lie down and starve. The principal recommendations of the commissioners were based on the principle that the then existing system of poor laws was " destructive to the industry, forethought, and honesty of the labourers, to the wealth and morality of the employers of labour and the owners of property, and to the mutual goodwill and happiness of all." The commissioners declared that the system " collects and chains down the labourers in masses, without any reference to the demand for their labour ; that while it increases their numbers it impairs the means by which the fund for their subsistence is to be reproduced, and impairs the motives for using those means which it suffers to exist; and that every year and every day these evils are becoming more overwhelming in magnitude and less susceptible of cure." The evils, they held, might be at least diminished by the combination of workhouses, and by a rigid administration and practical management instead of the existing "neglect, extravagance, robbery, and fraud." An alteration or abolition of the law of settlement might, the commissioners thought, save a great part or the whole of the enormous sums now spent in litigation and in removals, and allow the labourers to be distributed according to the demand for labour. They suggested that no relief should be given to the able-bodied or to their families except in return for adequate labour, or in a well regulated workhouse; that thereby a broad line would be drawn between the independent labourers and the paupers; that the number of paupers would be immediately diminished in consequence of the reluctance of persons to accept relief on such terms; and that pauperism would in the end, instead of forming a constantly increasing proportion of the population, become a small and well-defined part of it, capable of being provided for at less than half the amount of the existing poor rates. Finally, the commissioners recommended that the administration of the poor laws should be entrusted to the general superintendence of one central authority with extensive powers.

A Bill framed on these recommendations and embodying them as nearly as possible, was introduced into Parliament. It naturally created a very strong opposition. There was everything in the proposed measure which could raise up against it all the sentimental feelings that tend to foster and cherish pauperism. Beggary had been so long an institution of the country that many persons

had come to regard it with a sort of kindly feeling, and
had been accustomed to think that the relation between
the mendicant and the donor was of a mutually improving kind, something like that between a good master
and a faithful servant. All that sort of easy benevolence
by which we each of us feel inspired now and then
when we are inclined to throw coppers among whining
beggars in the street, raised itself in opposition to the
somewhat stringent policy of the Government. The
measure was, however, passed almost in its integrity
through both Houses. The Duke of Wellington was
liberal enough to give it his strong support, and to protest against the efforts of some of his own party in the
House of Lords to oppose the Bill, in consequence of the
lateness of the period at which it was introduced. It
was carried into law, and we believe we may safely state
that on the whole the hopes with which it was introduced
have been well-sustained and the prophecies of evil have
come to nothing. Many and various defects indeed have
been found since that time and still exist in the working
of the poor law. Many changes have been made which
deviate a good deal from the rigid principle of self-
dependence on which it was introduced. The administration of outdoor relief in large towns is still a source of
much corruption and demoralisation. But it would be
hardly possible to administer such a system with any
regard to mercy, not to say generosity, and not at the
same time to open the door to fraud and to depravity.
In great towns it very often happens that the poor law
officials, acting sternly in some particular case where
they suppose relief is not really needed, make a complete
mistake and deny assistance exactly where it is most
imperatively required. Some poor creature dies at the
door of a workhouse to which he or she has just been

K

refused admission. Some old woman sends a pathetic apeal to the relieving officers; they disbelieve her story or neglect the appeal, and after a while she is found by her neighbours dead from sheer starvation in her miserable garret. Then a natural outcry is raised by the public. The feelings of every humane person are touched and the impression goes abroad that the workhouse officials are hardened against all sense of pity. A relaxation in their system naturally takes place, and for a while outdoor relief is heedlessly given to almost anyone who asks for it. These, however, are only some of the casual defects of a system which by its very nature could hardly be so administered as not to fall into error every now and then. No one, we believe, will deny that on the whole the change in the poor law system made by Lord Grey's Government was wise and just, and has been attended with results even more satisfactory than those which its promoters might at one time have felt themselves entitled to expect.

In 1835 Lord Melbourne's Government just settled firmly in office, took on themselves the task of reforming the whole system of municipal corporations. Lord John Russell had charge of the Bill which was to accomplish this object. The reform of the municipal corporations was a necessary sequel to the reform of the House of Commons itself. Petitions for reform had been pouring in from all manner of places, and Lord Althorp some years before had moved for a select committee to inquire into the state of municipal corporations in England and Ireland and Wales. Scotland was not included within the terms of the inquiry, because it was understood that Lord Jeffrey, as Lord Advocate, would undertake to deal with the Scotch boroughs himself. The committee recommended the appointment of a commission capable of making inquiries locally into the state of each separate corporation. The inquiry began in 1833, and was not finished until after the opening of Parliament in 1835. The Report was a very interesting contribution to history. It traced the whole growth of the municipal corporation in this country. It showed how the institution began by the collecting together of a few men within a certain limited space, in order to carry on in security the humble trades by which they lived. All around them the great majority of their fellow-countrymen were the mere serfs of the local landlord. The traders found that a mere serf who had no rights of person or property which his landlord was bound to respect, could not with success carry on any trade or business. They therefore refused to admit the claims of the local magnate, and insisted on their right to personal freedom. Little colonies, brought together for the purposes of trade, became established in various parts of England, and were the first centres of personal and political liberty there. The man who had once proclaimed himself free, claimed the same right for his descendants. Not only that, but it was a condition of almost all these free settlements, that one who married a freeman's daughter should himself become a freeman. One who served an apprenticeship to trade became as free as his master when his time was out. When the traders thus formed themselves into little communities, they found it necessary to meet occasionally and talk over common measures. In time it was found that large public meetings could not serve the purpose, and so the affairs of each locality were entrusted to committees, and these committees gradually grew into what we now call local corporations.

Some of the English Sovereigns were especially

anxious to conciliate the traders, who had the means of assisting them in many ways. The Tudor monarchs began to grant charters of incorporation to certain of these communities. In some cases the whole bulk of the resident freemen formed the corporation, but in a greater number of cases only a small and chosen body was constituted a municipality. After a while it was understood that the corporations consisted only of the ruling body. The government of a corporation was generally vested in a chief magistrate and a town council. In many small places the mayor had the authority almost entirely in his own hands, and not uncommonly dispensed as he pleased the revenues of the municipality. After a while corruption began to creep into many of these institutions. Most of the town councils were self-elected, and the members held their seats for life. They spent their funds as they pleased. They increased the salary of officers who had nothing to do. They lavished money on entertainments to themselves and their friends. They let out the property of the borough to their own members at merely nominal rents. They made every possible use of their position and their power to promote the success of the political party to which the majority happened to belong. Customs, tolls, or dues, which they were chartered to collect for public purposes, were in some cases coolly converted by the corporations into private property. The corporations had all varieties of jurisdiction. They had local courts of the most various authority. In some large towns their local courts were not empowered to try any case of felony. In one or two very small places they had, on the contrary, the right to try capital cases, and even to pronounce the capital sentence. They had recorders in most cases to try criminal cases, but the recorder was

not always a lawyer. In some places the recorder allowed twenty years cr more to pass without taking the
trouble to visit the seat of his local authority. In his
absence the town clerk or somebody else tried the cases,
and it occasionally happened that the town clerk, or
other sub-deputy who acted in this capacity, was called
upon to act as judge in some case which nearly concerned the interests, if not of himself, at least of some
member of his family, or some partner in business.

Both the great English political parties made use of
the corporations, and with about equal recklessness, in
order to promote their political interests. When Lord
John Russell made an attack on the manner in which
the Tory party had used their influence over certain
rotten corporations, Sir Robert Peel retorted by describing the case of the corporation of Derby. In Derby, Peel stated, that whenever the Whigs thought that
the number of freemen in their interest was getting low,
the mayor or some other leading member of the corporation applied to the agents of the Cavendish family, and requested a list of the names of persons who might be admitted as honorary freemen. He also stated that on the
last occasion when this application was made, the honorary freemen were almost all of them tenants of the Duke
of Devonshire, and the fees on their admission were paid
by the Duke's agents. Indeed, it is hardly necessary to
point out that such a complicated, heterogeneous, and
irresponsible system as that on which most of the corporations were founded must necessarily lead to corruption. Where bodies of men are self-elected, where they
are empowered, or at least empower themselves, to administer without responsibility the revenues collected for
public purposes and the property which belongs to the
public ; where they can obtain exclusive commercial

and trading privileges, and assert for themselves the right to put in use the most various judicial authority; and where, in addition, they can make themselves political engines, and assist in every way the political party whose interests they desire to forward, it is not necessary to say that political and social corruption must be the inevitable result.

The Whig Government determined to deal resolutely with these abuses. Lord John Russell, now leader of the House of Commons, introduced his Bill on June 5, 1835, He proposed that it should apply to 183 boroughs not including the Metropolis, and containing an aggregate population of two millions of people, or an average of eleven thousand persons in each borough. In most cases he designed that the boundary of the parliamentary borough should be the boundary of the municipal borough likewise, and in a few cases the Crown was to have the right of defining the municipal borough. The governing body was to consist of a mayor and a council, and the councillors were to be elected by resident ratepayers. Twenty of the largest boroughs were to be divided into wards, and a certain number of councillors were to be elected by each ward. The rights of existing freemen were to be maintained, but as the freemen gradually died out the rights were to be extinguished. Exclusive trading privileges were to be abolished. The management of the charitable funds was to be entrusted to bodies chosen not from the council but from the ratepayers at large. The Crown was to nominate a recorder for each borough which was willing to provide a proper salary for the office, but the recorder was always to be a barrister of at least five years' standing. This seems to us now a very moderate measure of reform. It left a great many anomalies and abuses untouched. But at the time of the

introduction of the measure it was thought a most audacious attempt   It was regarded, to adopt a phrase that
afterwards became famous in politics, as "a gigantic
innovation.'

Sir Robert Peel followed Lord John Russell.   He
made a remarkable speech.   He did not oppose the introduction of the Bill.   On the contrary, he acknowledged the necessity for some sort of legislation on the
subject, but he took advantage of the opportunity to find
some fault with the Government scheme, and to make
known once for all his own opinion with regard to municipal reform.   It was clear that he had no intention of
acting the part of an obstructionist in regard to such
legislation.   He advised all members of corporations to
concur readily in the amendment of the existing system,
but on the express condition that there was to be a real
and genuine reform, and that the occasion was not to be
made a mere pretext for transforming power from one
party in the State to another.   What the country wanted,
he declared, was a good system of municipal government, taking security, as far as security could be taken,
that a really intelligent and respectable portion of the
community of each town should be called to administer
its municipal affairs, and that the future application of
the charitable or corporate funds should never be diverted
to any other than charitable and corporate purposes.
Sir Robert Peel was not unreasonable in the fear which
he expressed as to the possibility of municipal reform
being made the means of advancing the interests of one
party.   At that time we are afraid that few public men
had entirely emerged from the condition of political
development which makes it seem fair to take advantage of such an opportunity for such a purpose.   Mr.
O'Connell expressed his approval of the measure, but

said that the title of the Bill wanted one word which greatly diminished its value; it was called a Bill for the better regulation of Municipal Corporations in England and Wales. The word he wished to see introduced was " Ireland." It was shortly after stated that the Government intended to bring forward a Bill for Ireland of much the same nature as that for England and Wales.

The Bill was read a second time on June 15, without a division, and was in committee for not quite a month. The Conservative party had begun to understand that mere obstruction is of little use when a strong force of public opinion is behind those who introduce a measure. It is also right to say that the opposition was very much mitigated by the conduct of Sir Robert Peel, who set himself to work sincerely to make a good measure of municipal reform out of the Government scheme, and did his best to prevent anything like unnecessary resistance. The chief objection which the Conservative party raised was to the clause which declared that after the passing of the Act no person should be elected a citizen, freeman, liveryman, or burgess of any borough in respect of any right and title other than that of occupancy and payment of rates within the borough. The object of this clause was to get rid of the system which allowed the freedom of a borough, and with it the parliamentary and municipal franchise, to be acquired by birth, apprenticeship, purchase, marriage, or the favour of the corporation. These honorary freemen, as we may call them, had valuable privileges in many boroughs. They had rights of pasturage, or a share in the commons near the towns, and of the proceeds of the sale of common land, if there should be any sold. In other places they had the privilege to enter free of toll in any fair or market. In others they shared in the monopoly of trade which was enjoyed

by the resident freemen generally. An amendment was
moved by Sir William Follett, for the purpose of preserving the franchise for the freemen. Lord Grey had
very unwillingly allowed existing freemen to retain the
parliamentary franchise, and the clause in the Municipal
Reform Bill would put an end to the future admission of
freemen to that privilege. Sir William Follett insisted
therefore that the clause was really a new measure of
political reform, and contended that the Government
had already pledged themselves that their Reform Act
of 1832 was final. It was argued, with perhaps more
show of justice, that if the freemen were to be deprived
of the privilege which the Reform Bill allowed them to
retain, it should be done by a separate Act of Parliament
and not be brought in casually as a mere chance result
of the reorganization of the municipalities. The argument, however, of the Government and its supporters
against the whole system was clear and direct. The
freemen were not necessarily residents of the borough
or ratepayers. They had no natural interest in its affairs
or in its prosperity, and they were not open to the control of its public opinion. They regarded their privilege
in many cases merely as something to be sold. There
was no reason why a man who had been in prison might
not give a vote as well as the most respectable citizen.
It would be impossible to reform any municipality if
this class of persons were still to be allowed the control
of its affairs. On the other hand, if they were unfit to
exercise the municipal franchise, with what show of reason
could the Government allow them the right to vote for
members of Parliament? The amendment, and others
having the same object in view, were rejected. Mr.
Molesworth, in his "History of England," points out
that the Bill had "one most valuable, though indirect,

effect," which was not contemplated perhaps by its authors. "By putting an end," he says, "to the rights of
apprenticeship and exclusive trading, it struck off one
fetter on industry, as the poor law, in dealing with settlements, had struck off another. Both of them, by pre-
venting men from trading or working where they would,
interfered most mischievously with the freedom of labour."

Sir Robert Peel proposed that in the case of the larger
boroughs, members of the governing body should be required to have personal property to the value of 1,000*l*.,
or to be rated on a rental of not less than 40*l*. a year, and
that in the smaller boroughs the qualifications should be
a property of 500*l*., or a rated rental of 20*l*. a year. This
proposal, too, was rejected, and was, indeed, in direct
opposition to the spirit and purpose of the Bill. Mr.
Grote took advantage of the opportunity to move that
the ballot be employed in municipal elections. It is
almost needless to say that he was unsuccessful. Nearly
forty years more had to pass away, and the country had
to go through an unspeakable amount of political and
municipal corruption and degradation, before the mind
of England could be brought to perceive the value of the
system for which the historian of Greece pleaded so
patiently and so long. The Bill was sent up to the
House of Lords on July 21, without any material change
in its character. The majority there were, of course,
opposed to it. They had not the courage to reject it,
especially after the stand which had been taken by Sir
Robert Peel, but they determined to mutilate and mangle
it as much as they thought it would be safe to attempt.
The speech in which Lord Melbourne introduced the
Bill, probably rather encouraged than discouraged the
House of Lords in such a course. Lord Melbourne

was never a very earnest or resolute man, and he was already beginning to think that his administration was loosing a little of its hold on Parliament and the public. The House of Lords, therefore, took courage enough to introduce amendments into the Bill, virtually the same as those which the House of Commons had rejected. The Conservative peers with Lord Lyndhurst at their head went wild over the Bill. They seemed to have for the most lost their heads. They mutilated the Bill with reckless hands. They restored all, or nearly all, the anomalies which the Government had been endeavouring to abolish. They positively introduced entirely novel anomalies and fresh springs of abuse into it. They contrived to make it a Bill for increasing the stringency of religious tests. Of course the House of Commons could not accept such alterations. Peel strongly discountenanced the wild attempts of Lord Lyndhurst and the Tory peers. Wellington advised the Tories to give way, and at last even Lyndhurst himself had to offer counsel of the same kind. Lord John Russell on his side recommended the Commons to yield a few small and unimportant points. The Lords saw no way out of the difficulty but to submit, and on September 7, 1835, the Bill, substantially the same as when it left the House of Commons, became the law of the land.

CHAPTER X.

LEGAL AND SOCIAL REFORM.

ON June 20, 1837, King William IV. died. He had reigned but a short time. He came to the throne when he was already an old man. He had been a sailor, and a sailor of the roughest school, and in many of his opinions, as, for example, his views on the question of

the slave trade and slavery, he ran counter to the
feeling of the great majority of Englishmen. But on
the whole he had made a respectable constitutional
Sovereign, and during the struggles which ended in the
passing of the Reform Bill he had behaved with fairness and with prudence. His death was followed by
the accession of Queen Victoria to the throne. The
Princess Victoria was his niece. She was the daughter
of the Duke of Kent, fourth son of George III. William IV. left no child living when he died, and the
Crown therefore passed over to his niece, Victoria.

The Queen was born on May 24, 1819. She was
therefore little more than eighteen years of age when she
was thus suddenly called to a throne which, at her birth,
there could have been little expectation that she would
ever have to fill. She was named Alexandrina Victoria.
The name Alexandrina was given to her by her father,
in compliment to the Emperor of Russia. The intention
was that she should also bear the name Georgiana, after
her uncle, George IV., then Prince Regent. The Duke
of Kent, however, insisted that Alexandrina should be
her first name, and thereupon the Prince Regent declared
that the name of Georgiana could not stand second to
any other in the country, and that therefore she must not
bear it at all. It was, perhaps, fortunate on the whole
that the name of Georgiana was not given to the young
Princess. Its more recent associations were not of happy
omen; to perpetuate them would not have been welcome
to the country. The Queen had been carefully brought
up by her mother in almost absolute seclusion. None of
the statesmen or officials of the time had any close personal acquaintance with the young Princess, or any
reason to feel satisfied with regard to her opinions or her
capacity. The Duchess of Kent naturally desired seclu-

sion for the Princess, because neither at the Court of George IV. nor at that of William IV. were the manners of society such as to make a careful mother anxious that her daughter should see much of Court circles. The young Queen surprised everyone almost from the first moment when she came into public life by her composure, her force of character, and her intelligence. Yet so strong was the influence of party spirit, and so high did its passions run, that on both sides of the political field there were heard wild cries of alarm at the Queen's accession. On one side of the field, the clamour was that . the Tories were trying to bring about a revolution in favour of the Hanoverian branch of the Royal Family, that they were plotting to depose the Queen and put the Duke of Cumberland in her place. On the other side, the alarm-cry was that the Queen was sure to favour the Roman Catholics, that she would turn Catholic herself, or at the very least would marry a Catholic prince. The leading paper of that day thought it convenient and becoming to remind the Queen that if she were to turn Catholic or to marry a Catholic, she would immediately forfeit her crown. The Queen had not been many months on the throne when she satisfied every one that she was a thoroughly constitutional Sovereign, that she was capable of acting with absolute impartiality between Liberal and Tory, and that she had full capacity for the duties so suddenly imposed on her. In 1840, the Queen was married to her cousin, Prince Albert of Saxe-Coburg-Gotha, who afterwards received the title of Prince Consort.

One important result of the accession of Queen Victoria was the severance of the connection between this country and the kingdom of Hanover. Hanover had become connected with England, because it was ruled by the Prince who, after the death of Queen Anne, came to be Sovereign of this country.   But the law of Hanover limited the sovereignty to men, and therefore, when Queen Victoria succeeded to the throne of England, she did not become Queen of Hanover, but Hanover passed over to her uncle, the Duke of Cumberland, eldest surviving brother of William IV.   It was fortunate for England that she was thus disen angled from her connection with Hanover.   The Hanoverian connection had always been distasteful to most people here, and in times much more near to our own, England might have been involved in war if her Sovereign had still continued to be Sovereign of Hanover.   The great movement for German unity, which went on in later years, would hardly have been stayed by the existence of a kingdom of Hanover under what would have been practically a foreign Sovereign.   England would either have had to face the responsibility of maintaining Hanover against Germany or the discredit of surrendering it.

The reforms which were going on satisfactorily under a Sovereign so narrow-minded and uncultured as William IV., were not likely to be stayed in their course or to become less substantial in their character under the rule of a Queen so intelligent and liberal-minded as Victoria, On the contrary, the energy of reform seemed to grow in strength and to be guided with increasing enlightenment.   Apart from purely political questions, the great subjects of the reformer's interest when Queen Victoria came to the throne were the condition of national education, the criminal law, and the system of taxation.   It seems hard to believe now how stupid and barbarous were the principles on which, even up to the time of the Queen's accession, and for long after, the taxation of the country and its criminal law were carried on. Newspapers were taxed, as if people ought to be prevented from reading them; windows were taxed, as if it were the business of the Government to take care that men and women did not have too much air and sunlight in their houses. The window tax had been in existence for centuries, and about this time used to return more than a million of money every year to the revenue. A house was taxed according to the number of its windows, and the result of course was that householders reduced the number as much as possible, and the poorer a man was the greater was the necessity for his depriving his family of light and air. A common practice was to paint rows of windows on one of the solid walls of a house, so that the house might at least seem to the hasty passer-by to enjoy that light which the rigour of taxation denied it. Twenty years had yet to pass away before this odious tax was finally abolished.

Soon after the Queen's accession an attempt was made to establish something like a system of national education. The first movement that way had been made a few years earlier, in 1834. The movement then began by a grant of money for the purposes of elementary education. Twenty thousand pounds was the sum first given, and the same grant was made each successive year until 1839, when Lord John Russell asked for an increase of 10,000*l.*, and proposed a change in the way of distributing the money. At first the grant was given through the National School Society, a body in direct connection with the English Church, and the British and Foreign School Association, which admitted children of all denominations without imposing on them sectarian instruction. Lord John Russell obtained an order in council transferring the distribution of the money to a committee of privy council. The proposals of the Government were bitterly opposed in both Houses of Parliament. An application of the public money through the hands of the committee of the privy council, not in any sense under the direct control and authority of the State, was denounced as a State endowment of popery and heresy. The Government, however, succeeded in carrying their point, and established their Committee of Privy Council on Education, the institution in whose hands the management of the whole system of public instruction has rested ever since.

Some of the most effective and benign measures to mitigate the harshness of our criminal legislation were taken in this chapter of our history. The Custody of Infants Bill was one of the first legislative declarations that there is any difference between an English wife and a purchased slave woman, so far as the power of the master over either is concerned. The Custody of Infants Bill gave to mothers of irreproachable conduct, who, from no fault of their own, were living apart from their husbands, occasional access to their children, with permission and under control of the judges. It seems marvellous to us now to think that there ever could have been a time when such a measure met with resistance from rational human beings. Reforms were going on year after year in the criminal law. The severity of the death punishment was mitigated by successive Acts of Parliament. In 1832, capital punishment was abolished in cases of horse-stealing, sheep-stealing, coining, larceny to the value of 5*l.* in a dwelling-house, and other offences. In 1833, house-breaking ceased to be a capital crime. In 1834, a man who had escaped from transportation, and come back to this country, was no longer liable to the punishment of death. In 1835, letter-stealing by servants in the Post Office was removed from the black list of capital offences, One curious result of all these gradual reductions of the death penalty, has been to establish a much nearer proportion, in our days, between the number of persons sentenced to death and the number of persons actually executed. When the death sentence was made to apply to almost every offence that men or women could commit, it was impossible, seeing that human nature must then, as now, have had some compassion in it, that all these sentences, or even a considerable portion of them, could ever have been carried into effect. For example, in 1824, 1,066 persons were sentenced to death, of whom only 40 were executed. In the following year, 1,036 were sentenced and 50 executed. In 1837, 438 persons were sentenced to death, of whom only 8 were executed. But if we come down to milder times, we find that in 1860, 48 were sentenced and 12 executed. In 1861, 50 persons were sentenced and 15 executed. In the earlier years the number of executions is hardly 1 in 20 to the number of sentences, while, in the later years, it is sometimes 1 in 2. The superiority in the policy of our times is not merely its being a policy of greater mercy, but also in its being a policy of greater efficacy. If the death sentence is to have any influence at all in deterring from crime, its influence must be, in a great degree, by the certainty of its infliction. It is obvious, therefore, that a sentence of which there are 15 inflictions out of 50 condemnations, must be more effective as a deterrent than a sentence which is only inflicted 40 times in 1,066 cases of its delivery. The question whether the death penalty ought to be inflicted at all, whether its deterring effect is really so considerable as to render it worth retaining the punishment, is one of great public interest and im-

L

portance, but into which it is not necessary at present to enter. The point on which we desire particularly to insist is, that not only have our modern principles mitigated the action of the death penalty, but they have, at the same time, so applied it as to render its deterrent effect, if it has any, more distinct and operative than it could have been in days less humane.

How to deal with criminals not sentenced to the death penalty, or on whose behalf that penalty had been mitigated, was a question which occupied the attention of Parliament during many successive years. The system of transportation had grown to be an intolerable nuisance to our rising colonies. Transportation, as a systematised means of getting some of our criminals out of our way, began in the time of Charles II. The judges then gave power for the removal of criminals to the North American colonies. The colonies, however, as they grew into civilisation and strength, began to protest against this use being made of their soil, and of course the revolt of the North American provinces, and the creation of the United States of America, rendered it necessary for England to send her convicts to some other part of the world. In 1787 a cargo of criminals was sent to Botany Bay, on the eastern shore of New South Wales. Afterwards, convicts were sent to Van Diemen's Land and to Norfolk Island, a solitary island in the Pacific, 800 miles, or thereabouts, from the shores of New South Wales. Norfolk Island has been described as the penal settlement for the convicted among convicts, that is to say, criminals, who having been transported to New South Wales committed new crimes there, might be selected by the colonial authorities, and sent for severer punishment to Norfolk Island.

There had been growing up in this country an impression for a long time that the transportation system was the parent of intolerable evils. It had been condemned by Romilly and Bentham. In 1837, the House of Commons appointed a committee to consider the whole question. Amongst others on the committee were Sir Robert Peel, Lord John Russell, Mr. Charles Buller, Sir William Molesworth, and Lord Howick, afterwards Earl Grey. The evidence put before that committee disclosed a number of horrors which made it certain that the transportation system must come to an end. Norfolk Island, as we have said, was kept for the convicted among the convicts. A number of men, thoroughly brutalised, were left there to herd together like beasts. They worked, when they did work at all, in chains. They were roused at daybreak, turned out to labour in their chains, and allowed to huddle back to their dens when dark had set in. In Sydney, the convicts received, after a certain period of probation, a conditional freedom, or what we have lately called a ticket-of-leave. They were allowed to work for the colonists. Anyone requiring labourers or servants could apply to the authorities and have male or female convicts assigned to him to do his work. These convict labourers and servants were hardly better in condition than slaves. They were assigned over to masters and mistresses, for whom they had to work as ordered, and whose commands, however capricious, they had to obey. A special code of laws existed for the discipline of these unfortunate creatures. They moved about openly in the ordinary life of the place, working in trades, acting as domestic servants, labouring in the fields. They were living under conditions unknown to civilised life elsewhere. On the complaint of a master or mistress, men could be flogged with as many as fifty lashes for ordinary disobedience.

After a while, of course, they lost all hope of reform, all sense of decency. Their lives were alternations of profligacy and punishment. The worse a man was, the better he was likely to be able to endure such an existence. Indeed, a genuine, downright, irreclaimable scoundrel often liked well enough the kind of life he found in New South Wales. He had ample opportunity for profligacy, and as long as he obeyed the immediate orders of his master or mistress, he was not likely to be flogged. Sometimes the wives of convicts went out to the colony, started some business or some farming work there, and had their husbands assigned to them as servants. It is shown in the evidence that in a certain number of instances the women, probably to pay off old scores, took occasion now and then to have their husbands flogged. The publication of the report of the committee filled the public mind with so much horror that it was evident to all persons that the abandonment of transportation was only a question of time. The colonists themselves in most places began to interfere and to protest against it. At last it came so far that only in Western Australia were residents willing to receive convicts on any conditions, and Western Australia had little opportunity of receiving many of our outcasts, The finding of gold in Australia settled at last the question of these colonies being made any longer places for the shooting of our human rubbish. It would be impossible to send out shiploads of criminals to a region full of the temptations of gold. Various projects were formed of starting convict settlements in other places, but in every case some clear objection arose, and although for many years after, committees of both Houses of Parliament reported in favour of some sort of transportation system, they also recorded their conviction that it would be impossible to carry on the existing system any longer. Its death sentence was passed when the report of the commission was published.

It would not be right, in surveying the political and social improvements which belong to this period, not to speak of the great advantage secured for peace and order in towns and cities, and indeed everywhere over the country, by the organization and development of the police system. The London police force, remodelled by Sir Robert Peel, and constructed very much as we now know it, began its duty about the time when this history opens. Before that time there had only been a miserably inefficient watch system, the sport of satirists, and not at all the terror of evil-doers. The Metropolitan organization became the model for the police force of all the great towns of England and Scotland, and for the capital of Ireland. But the police force of Ireland in general is a semi-military body, embodied to deal with a condition of things entirely different from that which exists in England.

A few words may be given to the small but very important reform effected in the interests of humanity by the suppression of the practice of sending boys up chimneys to clean them. The trade of the chimney-sweep pursued in this way was unknown, we believe, to any country except in England. It began in England about the beginning of that eighteenth century whose ways have lately occupied so much of our attention, and called forth so many more or less unsuccessful attempts at imitation. Most of the chimneys of the English houses were narrow and crooked, and it was for a long time held as an article of faith that there was no efficient way of cleansing them except by sending a poor boy to climb from the fireplace to the top of the chimney, and proclaim that he had

accomplished his task by crying " sweep," when his soot-
covered head and shoulders emerged into the open air.
Nothing could have been more brutal than the treatment
of these poor climbing boys. Their hands, arms and
knees were abrased and injured by the constant friction
against the walls of the chimney. It sometimes happened
that the boy was sent up before the chimney had had
time to cool after the extinction of the fire, and then the
poor creature ran the risk of being severely burnt.
Sometimes he was severely burnt, Frequently the chimney was narrow and the child stuck fast in it, and was
only rescued with much trouble. In certain cases the
boy when taken out was found to be dead. Most people
had grown so familiarised with this abominable habit that
it never occurred to them to think of the suffering of
the poor creatures whom they saw sent up into their
chimneys—sometimes forced to go up by threats and
blows from the master sweep. At last, however, humane
persons began to call attention to the evil, and then an
agitation set in against it. Evidence was brought before
the public to show that in some cases where a boy had
stuck fast, the master sweep insisted that he was lazy
and perverse, and lit a fire in the grate in order to force
the poor creature to climb. It was shown that in several
instances the master sweeps had employed little girls
where they could not easily get boys, and it was stated
in Liverpool that a case was discovered in which a master
sweep for many years employed his wife, a young and
small woman, to do the work of a climbing boy. The
barbarous practice was suppressed by legislation in 1840,
but for a considerable time after its legal suppression it
continued to be secretly practised, in some places practised with almost no pretence of secrecy. Finally, public
opinion became thoroughly awakened to the horrors of

the whole system, and the practice of using climbing boys fell into absolute disuse. Chimneys now are built to suit a rational and humane system, and the sweeping machines have been found to do their work far better than even the most patient and energetic poor little boy who ever was victimized in the early days.

Among the earlier reforms of this period we must not omit to mention one which abolished a great grievance that had long supplied themes for the romancist, the poet, and the painter, and even still continues occasionally to supply them. This was the abolition of the law of impressment for the navy. The law of impressment, rather indeed a custom than a law, was of the most ancient practice. In the days of Richard II. it was spoken of as a system long in existence and well known. It was, however, regulated by a great variety of Acts of Parliament in various times, but by no possible regulation could it be anything except a monstrous grievance. From Richard II.'s time, through Philip and Mary, Elizabeth, William III., Anne, George II. and George III., Acts of Parliament had been passed for its regulation and restriction. The principle simply was that when the Government required seamen to carry on a war, they would take them where they could get them. The seaport towns were of course the place where they sought them, and sailors in the merchant marine were the men preferred for service on board ship. Our literature is full of pathetic stories of young seamen pressed as they were returning from the church where they had been married, and carried off to serve the Sovereign on the seas, perhaps not to return during many long years, perhaps not to return at all. There is, we believe, at least one true story of a seaman who was thus carried off after his wedding, who served all through the long stretch of the

war between France and England, and who returned a
man of more than middle age, to find his wife long since
dead, and himself a forgotten stranger in the home of his
youth.   Sometimes the carrying out of the impressment
service led to serious riots.   In Captain Marryat's once
popular novels there are given descriptions, which we
doubt not are true in the main, of the difficulties which
attended sometimes the capture of seamen for His
Majesty's fleet.   We read of serious resistance offered in
some of the lower quarters of Portsmouth, and of the
women joining in the fray, and seamen being dangerously
wounded, of shots fired from windows, of a stubborn
resistance made from room to room, and at last of the
objects of the search being captured and carrried off
much as the remnants of a stubborn garrison might be
taken by storm.   Many anti-reformers of that time
thought, as anti-reformers have always done when any
improvement is proposed, that it would be utterly impossible to carry on the service if the power to impre s seamen was not allowed to remain in the hands of the
authorities.   The press-gang was, however, abolished by
a Bill which the Government brought in in 1835, and
which limited compulsory service to five years in the
navy.   Since that time Governments have again and
again been occupied in the consideration of measures to
supply the navy with a sufficient stock of seamen, and
also to maintain a good naval reserve.   The first step,
however, to maintaining a really respectable body of men
in the service, was taken when the Government abolished
the press-gang.   So long as that system existed it was
not practically possible to do away with the flogging
discipline.   The men who were snatched up and pressed
for service on board ship were not likely at first to settle
down quietly to all the proper discipline and organization

of the navy. Sometimes the press-gang carried off men who were but the scum of the seaport towns, hardly better than the gaol bird class. One or two of these men impregnated with his bad habits half a forecastle full of sailors, and it is fairly to be acknowledged that very stringent measures of discipline were sometimes required to keep such persons in order. The abolition of the press-gang system rendered possible the abolition of flogging, and one can hardly believe that there can be any serious difficulty, by wise and liberal measures on the part of the Government, to maintain an excellent naval reserve, and to induce a good class of men to enter that naval service which has been always so especially popular among the English people.

One of the greatest social reforms accomplished during all this time was the change in the postal system. For a long succession of years the charge for the delivery of letters through the post had amounted to a practical exclusion of all the poorer classes from its substantial benefits. The rates of postage had been high and varied. They varied with regard to distance and with regard to the weight and even the size or shape of a letter. There was a London district post which was a distinct branch of the whole department, and with a different scale for the transmission of letters. The average charge on every letter throughout the kingdom was a little more than 6*d*. A letter from London to Brighton cost 8*d*., from London to Aberdeen 1*s*. 3*d*., from London to Belfast 1*s*. 4*d*. As if this tax was not enough, there was an arrangement that if the letter included more than one sheet of paper it should, no matter what its weight, come under a higher rate of charge. Members of Parliament could send letters free through the post to a certain extent; members of the Government could send them through without

limit. The country has now almost forgotten the franking system. Few people remember the time when the
name of a Member of Parliament scrawled upon the
outside of a letter sent it free through the post. It was
not alone the member's own letter or letters which thus
went free. Any letter which he endorsed with his name
was entitled to the same privilege. In other words, people
who could best afford to pay for their letters sent them
without charge, and those who could least afford to pay
anything had to pay a double rate, that is, to pay for the
transmission of their own letters and to make good the
deficiency in the postal revenue caused by the privilege
conferred upon the class who would send their letters free
of charge. In the years between 1815, that is, immediately after the close of the great war, and 1835, the
population of this country had increased 30 per cent.
The stage-coach duty has increased 128 per cent. In
other words, the population has increased by nearly a
third, and the amount of travelling done by stage-coach
had more than doubled itself. All this time the revenue
of the Post Office had remained stationary. In most
other countries, if not in all, the postal revenue had been
steadily increasing. In the United States the postal
revenue had trebled itself, although the American
system of posting was full of inconveniences and defects,
which might themselves have been thought sufficient to
prevent a great increase in the transmission of letters.

The extravagant system prevailing in England did
not merely interfere with the correspondence of the
public. It did that which all other unreasonable restrictions have the effect of doing, it created illicit
organisations for the purpose of defeating the law.
Enterprises for the transmission of letters privately, at
lower rates than those charged by the government,

sprang up everywhere. It is said that the owners of almost every kind of public conveyance were concerned in this traffic. Five out of every six of all the letters that passed between London and Manchester were believed to have been carried for many years by this unlawful process. Some great commercial firms sent fifty letters by this secret means of despatch for every one on which they paid the Government tax. The system was inquisitorial in its operation. An additional tax was laid on where a letter was written on more sheets of paper than one, and the post office officials kept up a frequent tampering with the seals of letters in order to find out whether or not they ought to be charged according to the higher rate. Mr. Hill, afterwards Sir Rowland Hill, is the man to whom we all owe the adoption of that uniform system which since his time has been adopted by every civilised state. A remarkable member of a remarkable family, Mr. Hill inherited social reform from his ancestors, and breathed in its spirit from the atmosphere around him. A story which Coleridge used to tell, called his attention to the unreasonableness of the post office system. Coleridge once, in the lake district, saw a postman deliver a letter to a woman at a cottage door. The woman looked at it but handed it back, declining to pay the postage, which was a shilliing. Coleridge heard her say that the letter was from her brother. He paid the shilling for her, in spite of a certain demonstration of objection on her part. When the postman had gone she explained to Coleridge that he had wasted a shilling. There was nothing in the letter. Her brother and she had agreed long before that while all was well with him he was to send a blank sheet once a quarter, and she thus had news of him without paying the postage. This at once struck Mr. Rowland Hill as a proof that there must be something fundamentally wrong in the system which drove a brother and sister to cheat the revenue, in order to gratify the reasonable desire to hear of each other's welfare. He set himself at once to work out a comprehensive plan of reform, which he laid before the world early in 1837. The essence of his plan lay in the principle that the cost of the conveyance of letters through the post was but trifling, and was but little increased by the distance over which they had to be conveyed. His idea was that the rates of postage should be reduced to the minimum, that the speed of conveyance should be increased, that there should be a greater frequency of despatch, and that there should be a uniform charge for the whole of the United Kingdom. The strongest opposition, both official and otherwise, was made to this scheme. The Postmaster-General, Lord Lichfield, declared it the wildest and most extravagant project he had ever heard of. He said the mails would be unable to carry the letters, that the walls of the post office would burst, and that the whole area on which the building stood would not contain the clerks and the letters. This, one would think, was the most unlucky argument against such a scheme. In order to show that Mr. Hill's plan ought not to be adopted, Lord Lichfield contended that the public would rush eagerly to avail themselves of its advantages. Not only officials opposed it. Even Sydney Smith declared it a nonsensical scheme.

Mr. Hill, however, persevered, and raised a great amount of public opinion in his favour. His plan was referred to a commission, who were engaged in inquiring into the whole conduct of the post office department, and they reported in its favour, although there was a general impression that it must involve a considerable loss of revenue. Mr. Hill's idea was that one penny the half-ounce should be the limit of charge within the United Kingdom. The Government took up the scheme at last and determined to run the risk. The commercial community of the great towns generally had been naturally much attracted towards the project. The Government determined to bring in a Bill to provide for the introduction of the scheme at once, and to abolish the franking system, except in the case of official letters sent on business belonging directly to Her Majesty's service. The proposal of the Government was that the rate of postage should be 4*d.* for each letter under half-an-ounce in weight, anywhere within the limits of the United Kingdom, but that this was to be only a beginning, for with the opening of January, 1840, the postage was to be a uniform rate of one penny per letter not beyond half-an-ounce in weight.

The introductory measure was passed in both Houses of Parliament. The Duke of Wellington declared that he strongly objected to it, but that as the Government evidently were determined to have it, he did not like to recommend the House of Lords to offer it any strong opposition. In the Commons Sir Robert Peel opposed it, and declared that it must involve the country in an immense loss of revenue. It was, however, passed into law. We need hardly say that it has not involved a loss of revenue, but that on the contrary the post office has been the best paying department under the whole charge of the Government since that time. In the last year of the heavy postage, 1839, the number of letters delivered in England and Ireland was rather more than eighty-two millions, five millions and a half as franked letters which returned nothing to the revenues of the State. In 1875 the delivery in the United Kingdom amounted to more than one thousand millions of letters. During that time, it is necessary to observe, the population has not nearly doubled itself. The population has not doubled, while the increase in the delivery of letters is as twelve to one. Every other civilised country has since adopted this system, and at the present time a letter is carried from London to San Francisco at a rate less than one-third of the cost of sending a letter from London to Brighton under the old system. Almost all the countries of the world have since come into an international postal system, by virtue of which a letter can be sent almost anywhere over Europe and all through the American States for $2\frac{1}{2}d$. There can be little doubt that fresh reductions will go on in this direction, and that probably before long the average penny will take a letter from London to Toronto or to Chicago as it takes it now from London to Dublin, The post-card system, first adopted in this country, has been a still further development of the same principle. We are, however, now anticipating by some years the limit which we have laid down for ourselves in describing this epoch of reform. But the change in the postal system may be said to have been accomplished in its entirety by the Act which came into force in 1840. The change from the fluctuating and extravagant scale to the uniform penny in this kingdom was the foundation and origin of all the reform that has since taken place. That once accomplished the rest followed.

It seems almost superfluous to point out that the new postal system could hardly have been developed to any considerable extent if it had not been for the sudden growth of the railway system throughout the country. The railway locomotive had been in use for some years before Rowland Hill made his first effort at postal re form. The railway had its beginning not in an attempt

to make public locomotion more quick and easy, but in
the humbler and narrower purpose of facilitating the
carrying of loads in colleries and other mines. These,
however, were not steam railways; they were something
like the tram-ways of our own days. There are disputes
as to the first inventor of the steam locomotive, just as
there are disputes about the original authorship of the
idea of a penny post, It is certain that George Stephenson was not the first man who got into his mind the
idea of a steam locomotive; it is quite possible that
some other man, that many other men, may have
thought of the uniform penny postal system before Rowland Hill. But in dealing with the history of any discovery or invention we must take as the author of a system the man who, not content with conceiving the idea
of it, was able to show how that idea could be carried
into effect, and who actually succeeded in making it a
reality. There is nothing ungenerous or unreasonable
in this. Hundreds of chance travellers may have talk-
ed of the possibility of piercing Mont Cenis in order to
make a railway tunnel under it; the world must regard
the man who put the idea into practical shape, and saw
that it was made a working reality, as the author of the
scheme for tunnelling the Alps. In the same way Rowland Hill and George Stephenson will always and justly
be looked up to as the originators of the railway system
and the cheap postal system. George Stephenson was
the son of a fireman in a Northumberland colliery, and
began life himself as an assistant fireman. Such education as he had he got at a night-school. He showed
from his childhood a genius for mechanics and inventions. He constructed his first locomotive engine in
1814: an engine which drew eight cars at the modest
rate of four miles an hour. A railway of his construc-

tion was opened between Stockton and Darlington in
1825, the first railway made for public use. Stephenson
was chief engineer of the Liverpool and Manchester
Railway, which was opened in 1830. The directors of
the railway offered a prize of 500*l.* for the construction
of the best locomotive, and the prize was won by George
Stephenson. His engine was called the " Rocket," and
ran at the rate of about thirty miles an hour. Stephenson's invention was met by every kind of objection, by
ridicule, by grave argument, by the criticism of men who
professed to be above all things practical, and by the
alarmist views of men who knew nothing about the subject. The opening of the line between Manchester and
Liverpool in 1830, was made memorable by the death of
Mr. Huskisson, an eminent English statesman. Huskisson had been in the Cabinet of the Duke of Wellington, had quarreled with his leader and had resigned.
They met again for the first time at one of the stations
near Liverpool, on the occasion of the opening of this
line of railway. The train stopped, and many of its
passengers got out of the carriage and walked on the
platform. Huskisson saw the Duke of Wellington, and
the Duke of Wellington made a movement towards him.
Huskisson hurried to respond to the apparent invitation,
and in endeavouring to reach the Duke, was struck by
the moving train and killed.

Nothing can be more remarkable than the change
which the railway brought about in the conditions of
travel. No change made since men began to travel
down to the invention of the railway was of any marked
importance. An Englishman travelling from London
to Rome during the early part of the reign of King William IV., would have travelled exactly as one of the Roman generals would have done who left England for

Rome in the days of the Cæsars. In each case the traveller would have had all the speed that horses and sails could give and no more. A traveller in Victoria's reign is borne with a speed which to our ancestors would have seemed like that of the wind, and by means of an agency which during long centuries had never occurred to the imagination even of enthusiasts and dreamers as a possible means of locomotion.

Still more marvellous than the railway is the electric telegraph. The authorship of this wonderful discovery and application is, like that of the railway and the postal system, still in dispute. In 1837 a patent was taken out by two Englishmen, Professor Wheatstone and Mr. Cooke, for a plan of transmitting messages by means of an electric current sent along a wire. In the very same year Professor Morse, an American electrician, made application to the Congress of his country for some aid towards the construction of a telegraph of a similar kind, and he was refused. He sought to take out a patent in England the year after, but he had come too late. Wheatstone and Cooke had been beforehand with him. It is likely enough that the same idea may have occurred to other men before Wheatstone or Cooke or Morse ; but we must regard Wheatstone and Cooke as practically the authors of that marvellous system of communication which sends words over far distances almost as quickly as man's thoughts can traverse them ; which has grown from a local into a national and from a national into an international system ; which brings London and Edinburgh closer for the interchange of message than the east and west ends of Fleet Street were fifty years ago, and lately has brought London and San Francisco, London and Melbourne, London and Calcutta, as close together as London and Edinburgh.

M

CHAPTER XI.

THE STOCKDALE CASE.—IRISH EDUCATION.

THE famous trial of Stockdale *v.* Hansard raised a very important point of law, which, however, it did not conclusively settle. It brought up the question how far the protection of the House of Commons will extend to secure immunity against libel for a publisher. At one time the case not only occupied the most serious attention of the House of Commons and of the country, but threatened to bring the Commons into something like permanent antagonism with the Courts of Law. Parliament had passed a Bill appointing inspectors of prisons, and these inspectors were desired to report annually on the condition of each prison which they visited. In their first report they mentioned that they had found in Newgate a book published by the Messrs. Stockdale, which they considered to be indecent and obscene. The opinion of the inspectors was published in the ordinary Parliamentary reports which Messrs. Hansard issued. We need not discuss the merits of the publication itself. It seems to have been a book on a subject very proper and necessary for the study of medical men and medical students, but which had no particular business amongst the literature furnished in prisons. Stockdale brought an action against Hansard for publishing the report, and insisted that the publication was libel. Hansard pleaded that the publication was privileged and that the statement was true. The case came before Lord Denman, Chief Justice of the King's Bench, in February, 1837. The jury found the libel justified by the character of the

work itself, and therefore brought in a verdict for the
defendant on the second issue which he had raised.
This way of dealing with the question got rid of the
difficult point as to privilege, so far as the jury were concerned. The Chief Justice, however, himself called attention to that issue, and declared that whatever arrangement the House of Commons might make with any
publishers, anyone who published a statement which
might be injurious or ruinous to one of His Majesty's
subjects, " must answer in a court of justice to that subject
if he challenges him for that libel." The House of Commons could not sit down quietly under such a ruling as
this. On the motion of Lord John Russell, it resolved
" that the power of publishing all such reports, visits, and
proceedings, shall be necessary as an essential incident
to the constitutional functions of Parliament ; that by the
law and privilege of Parliament the House of Commons
has the sole and exclusive jurisdiction as to the existence
and extent of its privileges, and that for any court or
tribunal to decide upon matters of privilege, inconsistent
with the determination of either House of Parliament, is
a breach and contempt of the privileges of Parliament."

Stockdale was not disturbed by this resolution. He
bought a second copy of the report of the prison inspectors, and brought a second action against the publisher.
The Attorney-General was directed to put a plea on record that Hansard had acted by the order of the House
of Commons. The four judges of the Court of Queens
Bench unanimously decided against the plea, and
Stockdale's damages were set down at a hundred pounds·
The House of Commons referred the matter again to a
committee. The majority of members of Parliament
thought the time had come for asserting the privileges of
the House, but Lord John Russell, Sir Robert Peel and

others, were inclined to get out of the dispute by yield
ing to the Law Courts. By a small majority, 184 votes
to 166, the House agreed to a motion proposed by Lord
John Russell and supported by Sir Robert Peel, pro-
mising to take proceedings for the purpose of staying
the execution of judgment. Stockdale, however, was
not content with his victory, but in 1839 he went to
Hansard's once more, bought a third copy of the Prisons
Report, and brought a third action against the publishers. He was awarded 600*l.* damages and 40*l.* costs.
The Sheriffs of London were called upon to seize and
sell some of the property of the Hansards to satisfy the
demands of the plaintiff. The money was paid into the
Sheriffs' Court under protest, in order to avoid the
scandal of a sale. The House of Commons ordered the
Sheriffs to refund the money to the Hansards. The
Court of Queen's Bench was applied to for an order
directing them to pay the money over to Stockdale. The
Sheriffs were finally committed to the custody of the
Serjeant-at-Arms, for contempt of the House of Commons. The Court of Queen's Bench at once served a
writ of *habeas corpus*, calling upon him to release the
Sheriffs. The House directed the Serjeant-at-Arms to
inform the Court that he held the Sheriffs in custody by
order of the Commons. The Serjeant-at-Arms conducted the Sheriffs to the Court of Queen's Bench and
made his explanation there. The explanation was declared reasonable, and he was allowed to conduct his
prisoners back again. The whole affair was becoming
ridiculous and humiliating. Not only did Stockdale
persevere with his actions, but numbers of other men,
fired by his example, continued to bring actions for
publications reflecting on them and contained in
official reports to the House of Commons. The public

in general sided with the Sheriffs and the Judges,
and against the authority of the House of Commons.
It must have been, one would think, owing in a great
measure to the defects of the Ministry itself, that
popular feeling went so much against them. The
House of Commons must have fallen strangely into dis-
repute when outsiders could regard its action in this
case, and even the principle on which its actions rested
as the overbearing conduct of a despotic House endeavouring to crush a few humble men. But the question
which the House of Commons sustained is, to us, one of
great importance. The view of the law on which Lord
Denman rested his ruling, was that Parliament has
power to protect any publications, but that the House of
Commons is not Parliament ; is only one of the estates
of the realm ; and therefore is not authorised to sanction
the publications of libels and to protect those who published them against the Courts of Law. But it seems
clear that to secure to each House of Parliament an
absolute authority and freedom of publication is of the
utmost importance to the least protected classes of the
community. No harm that could possibly come from
the undue exercise of such a privilege could be compared
to the evils which must arise from any restriction of the
rights of either House to publish whatever it thought
proper for the common good. Reform of any kind is
only obtained through freedom of debate and through
that publicity which freedom of debate secures. It would
not be of much avail to allow the utmost liberty of discussion in Parliament, as was done at all times, if the
publication of the debates were restricted, and thus the
sentiment of the country were never to be fully reached.
The poorer or humbler a man or a class may be, the
greater need is there for him to insist on full freedom

of publication by either House in Parliament. The abolition of slavery, the protection of factory children, the
putting down of the system which employed boys to
climb chimneys, the repression of the practice which
sent sailors to sea in vessels no better than rotten coffins,
all these are reforms which never could have been carried
but through the influence of public opinion, aroused by
the publication of debates and reacting on each House of
Parliament.

In the end the controversy was closed by a Bill
brought in by Lord John Russell on March 3, 1840, to
afford protection to all persons employed in the publication of Parliamentary papers. This Bill proposed that any
person against whom civil or criminal proceedings should
be taken on account of any such publication might bring
before the Court a certificate under the hand of the Lord
Chancellor or the Speaker, stating that it was published
by the authority of the House, and that the proceedings
should at once be stayed. This Bill, though it was
strongly opposed by lawyers in both Houses, was passed
quietly through, and became law on April 14. It settled
the question in a practical and simple way for the time,
but it did not define the relative rights of Parliament and
the Courts of Law. Since then, however, these rights
have practically defined themselves. It is now regarded
as settled that either House of Parliament may authorise
the publication in print of any document which it con-
siders necessary, and there will be no Stockdales found
in our days rash enough to attempt to found legal proceedings on such a charge. If any difficulty were again
to arise, it would then assuredly be necessary to define
and secure the privilege of either House of Parliament.
The difficulty, however, will in all probability not arise,
and the question may be regarded as at an end.

The Government made an attempt in 1865 to supply the defects of middle class education in Ireland. They started the scheme of the Queen's Colleges. The idea was to establish in Ireland three colleges for the purpose of diffusing higher education among the middle and upper classes, and indeed among all classes, high and low, who felt inclined to avail themselves of the institutions. The principle on which these colleges were to be conducted was that of a mixed education. They were to be open to all sects without distinction. Their honours, their offices, everything, were to be free of religious test. On the other hand religious teaching of any kind was to be excluded from them. They were to be secular in the strictest sense. One college was to be in Cork, one in Belfast, and one in Galway, and the whole were to be affiliated to an institution called the Queen's University, having an examining but no teaching power. At that time there was in Ireland only one University. That was the University of Dublin, with its one college, Trinity, the college being in many respects hardly distinguishable from the University. Trinity College, Dublin, had grown to be an essentially Protestant institution. It did indeed receive and educate Catholic young men, but it gave them none of its honours, and they could take part in none of its official work. Therefore, although young Catholics did resort to Trinity for the sake of education, it may be said that the Catholic body generally felt themselves shut out from its advantages. They were at all events at a very painful disadvantage. The Catholic young man, educated side by side with the Protestant in Trinity, was handicapped cruelly in his studies by the knowledge that he could not compete with his fellow students for any of the honours or rewards which the institution gave to mem-

bers of the Established Church. It was to supply this
very obvious defect, to get rid of this really national
grievance, that Sir Robert Peel, now in power, devised
the plan of the Queen's Colleges and Queen's University
in Ireland. Almost immediately on the scheme being
laid before the House of Commons, Sir Robert H. Inglis,
whom we have already mentioned in these pages, a Tory
of a school now passing quite away denounced the
scheme and branded the institutions by a name which
has clung ‚to them ever since, that of the "godless colleges." It afterwards came to be a common impression
that O'Connell was the man who stigmatised the colleges
with this name. Sir Robert Inglis, however, was the
inventor of the epithet. O'Connell afterwards adopted
it and gave it wider significance and popularity. Sir
Robert Peel's scheme brought him into direct opposition
with two great sections of the community, themselves
reciprocally antagonistic. The Protestants of the ex-
tremer order, and most of the Roman Catholics, joined in
condemnation of a system which proposed to omit religious teaching from national education. The colleges
were, however, founded, built, and carried on. Staffs of
teachers and professors were appointed. For a while it
seemed probable that the institutions would really
prosper and be popular. But after a time the heads of
the Roman Catholic Church met in synod and condemned
the principle of the institutions in the same sense that
Sir Robert Inglis had condemned it, and from that time
they may be said to have languished in Ireland. They
turned out some very successful scholars, not only
Protestants, but Catholics, and it is not unworthy of remark that some of their most successful students have
been most prominent in the attacks on the principle
which was the central point of their existence. But the

difficulty of education, that is to say, of a Government system of education, in a country like Ireland, was not to be solved by such a scheme as that of Sir Robert Peel. Looking at it with impartial eye, and removing oneself as far as possible from the mere sectarian's point of view, we cannot deny that the difficulty raised by the Roman Catholics is one of serious importance. It seems at the first glance a satisfactory and safe concession to freedom of religion if the State founds an institution which shall teach all classes and sects alike, independent of any religious test and free from the possibility of religious controversy. But then this can only be had under ordinary conditions by the virtual exclusion of religious teaching from the institution altogether. Here, then, is aroused the conscientious objection of those who declare that they would rather have no teaching at all than a mere secular teaching from which religious questions are excluded. Here the Protestants, or a large body of them, and the Roman Catholics joined hands. It seems clear that there is not a genuine religious equality in the system which offers education of a purely secular kind, alike to those who conscientiously approve of such a system of instruction and those who conscientiously disapprove of it. Successive Governments have been engaged in attempts to reconcile the system founded by Sir Robert Peel with the scruples of the Irish Roman Catholic population, and up to this time they have not succeeded. The importance to us in considering Peel's scheme is that it was at all events the first distinct admission on the part of the English Government that the Irish Roman Catholics were unjustly treated by the system which left to Ireland only one great University, and that of a distinctly Protestant character.

The debates which took place on the proposal to establish the Queen's Colleges were animated and in-

teresting.   Mr. Gladstone supported Sir Robert Peel
both by voice and by votes, but he resigned his office in
the Government shortly after, because of another attempt made by Sir Robert Peel to conciliate the Roman
Catholics.   This was the increase of the grant to the
Roman Catholic college of Maynooth in Ireland, a
college specially founded for the education of young men
who desire to enter the ranks of the priesthood.   Sir
Robert Peel was not the first to propose the grant.   From
a time preceding the Act of Union a grant of some kind
had been made to Maynooth.   Sir Robert Peel merely
proposed to make that sufficient which was then insuffi-
cient, to allow such a sum as might enable the authorities
of the college to keep it in repair and to accomplish the
purpose for which it was intended.   The proposal of the
Ministry created a fierce outcry all over the country.
There was really no question of principle whatever involved.   As Macaulay put it, there was no more principle at issue than there would be in the sacrifice of a
pound instead of a penny weight on some particular
altar.   Nearly half Peel's party in the House of Commons voted against his scheme on the second reading,
and Mr. Gladstone, then Vice-President of the Board of
Trade, resigned his place rather than support the
measure.   He had written a book on the relations of
Church and State, and he declared that he did not think
the views he had expressed in that work allowed him to
take any part in Sir Robert Peel's proposal for increasing the Maynooth grant   The measure was carried, but
it bequeathed a controversy which raged furious and
constant through the House of Commons and through
the country for some five-and-twenty years after.   When
the Maynooth grant was finally abolished, it was
abolished in a way which would little have satisfied

those who opposed it. It came to an end as a necessary consequence of the measure by which Mr. Gladstone abolished his State Church in Ireland.

The scheme of the Government for elementary education in Ireland had to contend against difficulties of a similar kind. For a long time the public teaching, such as it was, in Ireland had been conducted on the principle of what Mr. Walpole in his "History of England" describes very correctly as "protection in religion." The whole idea of public instruction for the Irish people was founded on the hope of its gradually and insensibly converting the populations to the Established Church. The idea was akin to that which commonly inspires a Government dealing with an alien race—the idea of gradually substituting the language of the conquerors for the language of the conquered. This latter difficulty, curiously enough, was one which never really came in the way of English rule in Ireland. No resistance was made to the substitution of the English language for the Irish. The change came about insensibly, without deliberate effort, and without any manner of serious objection. Charles Lever, the Irish novelist, has made a Greek girl in one of his stories express her wonder that the Irish people, even while striving to resist English ascendency, should yet make their speeches and sing their songs in the English language. No Greek, she says, would consent to speak at home in the tongue of the Turk. But the difficulty which did not exist in the matter of language, was thought by many statesmen easy to get over in the matter of religion. The true way, they thought, to make the Irish thoroughly loyal, was to gradually educate the Irish children in the tenets of the Protestant Church. It was for a long time forbidden by penal laws to any Irishman, a Roman Catholic, to avail himself of the services of a Catholic priest or a Catholic tutor for his children. The poorer classes either had to give up all idea of education for their children, or to send them to be taught in the Protestant Charter Schools. The Charter Schools were an entire failure. Howard, the great prison reformer, drew attention to some of the abuses in their administration, and early in the century, Royal commissions were appointed to inquire into that subject, and into the whole question of Irish education. In 1827 the information collected by these commissions was referred to a select committee. The select committee accepted in principle the recommendation of each commission. Each alike had laid it down as a principle that the instruction of the Irish people should not be joined with any attempt to influence the religious faith of any class of Christians. The select committee accepted the principle, and declared it to be of the utmost importance to bring the children of the different faiths together, so as to give them a common education on general subjects, and to leave them to be taught their religious faith under a separate system and under the control of their own guardians and ministers. In 1830 the committee on the condition of the Irish poor brought forward again the suggestion of the select committee on Irish education, and recommended its adoption in practice. It was then at last admitted, both by legislation and by public opinion, that the idea of converting the Irish, by forcing them to pass through Protestant Charter Schools, was a failure. Lord Stanley, as Chief Secretary for Ireland, had the task of introducing the first comprehensive Education Bill. This Bill proposed to establish a Board of National Education in Dublin, to be composed of Roman Catholic as well as Protestant members, and to have the control and direction of all the national schools, as they were

called, in Ireland—that is, the schools which were to
receive aid from the State. There had been for some
time in existence a private association called the Kildare
Place Society, which undertook to establish cheap schools
of its own, to assist other schools in various parts of the
country, and to educate teachers. It endeavoured to get
over the religious difficulty by giving no religious instruction in its schools, and only arranging that a portion of
the Bible should be read, without comment, each day.
The Government had been in the habit of giving a grant
to the Kildare Place Society. The society, however, was
not accepted by the Roman Catholics. They demurred
to any system of teaching which did not include distinct religious instruction, and which did not provide for
the interpretation of the Scriptures to Roman Catholics
by ministers of the Roman Catholic Church. Lord
Stanley now proceeded to transfer the grant formerly
given to the Kildare Place Society to the Board of
National Education which he was about to found, In
the schools under the Board, the children of every
religious denomination were to have a literary education together, and a separate religious instruction.
Selections only from the Bible were to be read in school
time, on two days in the week, and the Bible itself was
to be read before and after school hours on the other
days. Thus, those who wished to hear the Bible read
could hear it by coming before and remaining after
the regular hours, and those who desired Biblical instruction only from the ministers of their own church
could remain away. The objection raised to this scheme
came, in the first instance, from the Protestant side of
the controversy. Sir R. H. Inglis declared that the
Bible was rejected and insulted by any restrictive regulation, and demanded that the people should have the

Bible, the whole Bible, and nothing but the Bible. The attack, however, was not strong enough to prevent the Bill from being passed. The House agreed to a vote in aid of Lord Stanley's measure. For a while the new Board of Education worked very well. Archbishop Whately, the Protestant Archbishop of Dublin, and Archbishop Murray, the Roman Catholic prelate, were alike anxious to make the best they possibly could of the advantages placed within their reach, and sincerely desirous to spread through Ireland the benefits of a genuine national education. They both served upon the Education Board, and succeeded in effecting the compromise by which a copy of the Bible, with certain debatable passages omitted, might be read in schools attended alike by Roman Catholic and Protestant children. But the outcry was raised with renewed violence from both sides of the field of controversy. Dr. Phillpotts, a Protestant prelate, denounced the spending of public money on what he called the propagation of the Roman Catholic faith. It was complained that monks and nuns had been allowed to take charge of education in Ireland, and it was said that in one school certain Protestant children had been induced to remain and witness the eelebration of mass. On the other hand, Dr. MacHale, the Roman Catholic Archbishop of Tuam, condemned the compromise Bible, as we may call it, on which Dr. Whately and Dr. Murray had agreed, as a volume destructive to faith. The controversy, we may say, has gone on from that time to this. The difficulty of framing a common system of education, which shall include those who believe in secular education, and those who regard it as dangerous and odious, can hardly ever be completely got over. But there can be no doubt that, despite all differences and all objections, the national system of education then founded in Ireland has accomplished very great and valuable results. Viewed as a mere teaching system, some of its organisations were admirably adapted to convey to children a genuine knowledge of the subject, and not to teach them to repeat in parrot tones long words to which they attached no meaning. The Irish peasant child has naturally a taste for instruction, and where the teachers were adapted for the work, the schools were always successful in doing some substantial good. At all events, whatever modification or rearrangement may be adopted, now or at any future time, to meet religious scruples on either side of the controversy, it was an eventful epoch in the history of Ireland, when a Ministry agreed to establish a great popular system of education which should endeavour to deal fairly with the children of all faiths, and should not try to exalt one religious denomination at the expense of another.

CHAPTER XII.

FREE TRADE.

THE repeal of the corn laws was one of the greatest measures of reform passed in this long and busy period. The corn laws were the laws which imposed a duty on the importation of foreign grain into England. At one time this duty amounted practically to prohibition. In 1815, the celebrated Corn Law was passed, which was itself moulded on the Corn Law of 1770. By the Act of 1815, wheat might be exported upon a payment of 1s. per quarter customs duty, but the importation of foreign grain was practically prohibited until the price of wheat in England had reached 80s. a quarter, that is to say, until a certain price had been secured for the grower of grain at the expense of all the consumers in this country. It was not permitted to Englishmen to obtain their supplies from any foreign land, unless on conditions that suited the English corn-grower's pocket.

We may perhaps make this principle a little more clear, if it be necessary, by illustrating its working on a small scale and within narrow limits. In a particular street in London, let us say, a law is passed declaring that no one must buy a loaf of bread out of that street, or even round the corner, until the price of bread has risen so high in the street itself as to secure to its two or three bakers a certain enormous scale of profit on their loaves. When the price of bread has been forced up so high as to pass this scale of profit, then it would be permissible for those who stood in need of bread to go round the corner and buy their loaves of the baker in the next street; but the moment that their continuing to do this caused the price of the baker's bread in their own street to fall below the prescribed limit, they must instantly take to buying bread within their own bounds and of their own bakers again. This is a fair illustration of the principle on which the corn laws were moulded. The Corn Law of 1815 was passed in order to enable the landowners and farmers to recover from the depression caused by the long era of foreign war. It was "rushed through" Parliament, if we may use an American expression; petitions of the most urgent nature poured in against it from all the commercial and manufacturing classes, and in vain. Popular disturbances broke out in many places. The poor everywhere saw the bread of their family threatened, saw the food of their children almost taken out of their mouths, and they naturally broke into wild extremes of anger. In London there were serious riots, and the houses of some of the most prominent supporters of the Bill were attacked. The incendiary went to work in many parts of the country. At that time it was still the way in England, as it is now in Russia and other countries, for popular indignation to express itself in the frequent incendiary fire. At one place near London a riot lasted for two days and nights ; the soldiers had to be called out to put it down, and five men were hanged for taking part in it.

After the passing of the Corn Law of 1815, and when it had worked for some time, there were sliding scale acts introduced, which established a varying system of duty, so that when the price of home-grown grain rose above a certain figure, the duty on imported wheat was to sink in proportion. The principle of all these measures was the same. How, it may be asked, could any sane legislator adopt such measures ? As well might it be asked, how can any civilised nations still, as some still do, believe in such a principle ? The truth is, that the principle is one which has a strong fascination for most persons, the charm of which it is difficult for any class in its turn wholly to shake off. The idea is, that if our typical baker be paid more than the market price for a loaf, he will be able in turn to pay more to the butcher than the fair price for his beef: the butcher thus benefited will be enabled to deal on more liberal terms with the tailor ; the tailor so favoured by legislation will be able in his turn to order a better kind of beer from the publican and pay a higher price for it. Thus, by some extraordinary process, everybody pays too much for everything, and nevertheless all are enriched in turn. The absurdity of this is easily kept out of sight where the protective duties affect a number of varying and complicated interests, manufacturing, com-

N

mercial, and productive. In the United States, for example, where the manufacturers are benefited in one place and the producers are benefited in another, and where the country always produces food abundant to supply its own wants, men are not brought so directly face to face with the fallacy of the principle as they were in England at the time of the Anti-Corn Law League. In America Protection affects manufacturers for the most part, and there is no such popular craving for cheap manufactures as to bring the protective principle into collision with the daily wants of the people. But in England, during the reign of the corn law, the food which the people put into their mouths was the article mainly taxed, and made cruelly costly by the working of Protection.

Nevertheless, the country put up with this system down to the close of the year 1836. At that time there was a stagnation of trade and a general depression of business. Severe poverty prevailed in many districts. Inevitably, therefore, the question arose in the minds of most men in distressed or depressed places, whether it could be a good thing for the country in general to have the price of bread kept high by factitious means when wages had sunk and work become scarce. An Anti-Corn Law association was formed in London. It began pretentiously enough, but it brought about no result. London is not a place where popular agitation finds a fitting centre. In 1838, however, Bolton, in Lancashire, suffered from a serious commercial crisis. Three-fifths of its manufacturing activity became paralysed at once. Many houses of business were actually closed and abandoned, and thousands of workmen were left without the means of life Lancashire suddenly roused itself into the resolve to agitate against the corn laws, and

Manchester became the head-quarters of the movement
which afterwards accomplished so much. The Anti-
Corn Law League was formed, and a Free Trade Hall
was built in Manchester on the scene of that disturbance
which we have already described in these pages, and
which was called the massacre of Peterloo. The leaders
of the Anti-Corn Law movement were Mr. Cobden,
Mr. Bright, and Mr. Villiers. Mr. Cobden was not a
Manchester man. He was the son of a Sussex farmer.
After the death of his father he was taken by his uncle,
and employed in his wholesale warehouse in the city of
London. He afterwards became a partner in a Manchester cotton factory, and sometimes travelled on the
commercial business of the establishment. He became
what would then have been considered a great traveller, distinct, of course, from the class of explorers;
that is, he made himself thoroughly familiar with most
or all of the countries of Europe, with various parts of
the East, and with the United States and Canada. He
had had a fair, homely education, and he improved it
wherever he went by experience, by observation, and
by conversation with all manner of men. He became
one of the most effective and persuasive popular speakers ever known in English agitation. He was not an
orator in the highest sense. He had no imagination
and little poetic feeling, nor did genuine passion ever
inflame into fervour of declamation his quiet, argumentative style. But he had humour; he spoke simple,
clear, strong English; he used no unnecessary words.
He always made his meaning plain and intelligible,
and he had an admirable faculty for illustrating every
argument by something drawn from reading, or from
observation, or from experience. He was, in fact, the
very perfection of a common-sense talker, a man fit to

deal with men by fair, straightforward argument, to ex-
pose complicated sophistries, and to make clear the most
perplexed parts of an intricate question. He was exactly the man for that time, for that question, and for
the persuasive and argumentative part of the great controversy which he had undertaken.

Mr. Cobden's chief companion in the struggle was
Mr. Bright, whose name has been completely identified
with that of Cobden in the repeal of the Corn Laws.
Mr. Bright was an orator of the highest order. He had
all the qualifications that make a master of eloquence.
His presence was commanding ; his voice was singularly
strong and clear, and had peculiar tones and shades in
it which gave indescribable meaning to passages of anger, of pity, or contempt. His manner was quiet, composed, serene. He indulged in little or no gesticulation,
he had a rich gift of genuine Saxon humour. These
two men, one belonging to the middle class of the north,
one sprung from the yeomanry of southern England,
had as a colleague Mr. Charles Villiars, a man of high
aristocratic family, of marked ability, and indomitable
loyalty to any cause he undertook. Mr. Villiars for
some years represented the Free Trade cause in
Parliament, and Mr. Bright and Mr. Cobden did its
work on the platform. Mr. Cobden first, and Mr.
Bright after him, became members of the House of
Commons, and they were further assisted there by Mr.
Milner Gibson, a man of position and family, an effective debater, who had been at first a Conservative, but
who passed over to the ranks of the Free Traders, and
through them to the ranks of the Liberals or Radicals.
Every year Mr. Villiars brought on a motion in the
House in favour of Free Trade. For a long time this
motion was only one of the annual performances, which

by an apparently inevitable necessity, have to prelude
for many years the practical movement of any great
Parliamentary question. Mr. Villiers might have brought
on his annual motion all his life, without getting much
nearer to his object, if Manchester, Birmingham, Sheffield, Leeds, and other great northern towns had not
taken the matter vigorously in hand, if Cobden and
Bright had not stirred up the engergies of the whole
country, and brought clearly home to the mind of every
man the plain fact that reason, argument, and arithme-
tic, as well as freedom and justice, were distinctly on
their side.

The Anti-Corn Law League showered pamphlets,
tracts, letters, newspapers, all over the country. They
sent lecturers into every town, preaching the same
doctrine, and proving by scientific facts the justice of the
cause they advocated. These lecturers were enjoined to
avoid as much as possible any appeals to sentiment or
to passion. The cause they had in hand was one which
could best be served by the clear statement of rigorous
facts, by the simple explanation of economical truths
which no sophism could darken, and which no opposing
eloquence could charm away. The Melbourne Ministry
fell in 1841. It died of inanition : its force was spent.
Sir Robert Peel came into office. Mr. Cobden, who then
entered the House of Commons for the first time. seemed
to have good hope that even Peel, strong Conservative
though he was, might prove to be a man from whom the
Free Traders could expect substantial assistance. Sir
Robert Peel had, in fact, in those later years expressed
again and again his conviction as to the general truth
of the principles of Free Trade. "All agree," he said
in 1842, "in the general rule that we should buy in the
cheapest and sell in the dearest market." But he con-

tended that while such was the general rule, yet that various economical and social conditions made it necessary that there should be some distinct exceptions, and he regarded the corn laws and sugar duties as such exceptions. It may be mentioned, perhaps, that the corn laws had, in fact, been treated as a necessary exception by many of the leading exponents of the principles of Free Trade. Thus we have to notice the curious fact, that while Sir Robert Peel's own party looked upon his accession to power as a certain guarantee against any concession to the Free Traders, the Free Traders themselves were, for the most part, convinced that their cause had better hope from him than from a Whig Ministry.

The Free Traders went on debating and dividing in the House, agitating and lecturing all over the country, for some years without any marked Parliamentary success following their endeavours. An immense and overwhelming majority always voted against them in the House of Commons. They were making progress, and very great progress, but it was not that kind of advance which had yet come to be decided by a Parliamentary vote. Probably a keen and experienced eye might have noted clearly enough the progress they were making. The Whig party were coming more and more round to the principles of Free Trade. Day after day some Whig leader was admitting that the theories of the past would not do for the present, and, as we have said, the Tory leader had himself gone so far as to admit the justice of the general principles of Free Trade. At one point the main difference between Sir Robert Peel, the leader of the House of Commons, and Lord John Russell, the leader of the Opposition, seems to have been nothing more than this, that Peel still regarded grain as a necessary exception to the principle of Free Trade, and Lord

John Russell was not clear that the time had come when it could be treated otherwise than as an exception. An event, however, over which no parties and no leaders had any control, suddenly intervened to hasten the action and spur the convictions of the leaders on both sides, and especially of the Prime Minister. This was the great famine which broke out in Ireland in the autumn of 1845. The vast majority of the Irish people had long depended for their food on the potato alone. The summer of 1845 had been a long season of wet and cold and sunlessness. In the autumn the news went abroad that the whole potato crop of Ireland was in danger of destruction, if not already actually destroyed. Before attention had well been awakened to the crisis, it was officially announced that more than one-third of the entire potato crop had been swept away by the disease, and that the disease had not ceased its ravages, but, on the contrary, was spreading more and more every day. The general impression of those who could form an opinion was that the whole of the crop must perish. The Anti-Corn Law League cried out for the opening of the ports, and the admission of grain and food from all places. Sir Robert Peel was decidedly in favour of such a course. The Duke of Wellington and Lord Stanley opposed the idea, and the proposition was given up. Only three members of the Cabinet supported Sir Robert Peel's proposals— Lord Aberdeen, Sir James Graham, Mr. Sidney Herbert. All the others objected, some because they opposed the principle of the measure, and were convinced that, if the ports were once opened, they would never be closed again, which indeed was probably Peel's own conviction, and others on the ground that no sufficient proof had yet been given that such a measure was necessary. Lord John Russell, almost immediately after, wrote a

letter from Edinburgh to his constituents, the electors of
the city of London, in which he declared that something
must immediately be done, that it was "no longer
worth while to contend for a fixed duty," and that an end
must be put to the whole system of protection, as "the
blight of commerce, the bane of agriculture, the source of
bitter division among classes, the cause of penury, fever,
and crime among the people." This letter produced a
decisive effect on Peel. He saw that the Whigs were
prepared to unite with the Anti-Corn Law League in
agitating for the total repeal of the corn laws, and he
therefore made up his mind to recommend to the Cabinet an early meeting of Parliament, with the view to
anticipate the agitation which he saw must succeed in the
end, and to bring forward, as a Government measure,
some scheme which should at least prepare the way for
the speedy repeal of the corn laws.

A Cabinet council was held almost immediately after
the publication of Lord John Russell's letter, and Peel
recommended the summoning of Parliament in order to
take instant measures to cope with the distress in Ireland, and also to introduce legislation distinctly intended to prepare the way for the repeal of the corn laws.
Lord Stanley could not accept the proposition. The
Duke of Wellington was himself of opinion that the
corn laws ought to be maintained, but at the same time
he declared he considered good government for the
country more important than corn laws or any other con-
siderations, and that he was therefore ready to support
Sir Robert Peel's administration through thick and thin.
Lord Stanley and the Duke of Buccleuch, however,
declared that he could not be the parties to any legislation
which tended towards the repeal of the corn laws. Sir
Robert Peel did not feel himself strong enough to carry

out his project in the face of such opposition in the Cabinet itself, and he tendered his resignation to the Queen. The Queen sent for Lord John Russell, but Russell's party were not very strong in the country, and they had not a majority in the House of Commons. Lord John tried, however, to form a Ministry without a Parliamentary majority, and even although Sir Robert Peel would not give any pledge to support a measure for the immediate and complete repeal of the corn laws. Lord John Russell was not successful. Lord Grey, son of the Lord Grey of the Reform Bill, objected to the foreign policy of Lord Palmerston, and thought a seat in the Cabinet ought to be offered to Mr. Cobden. Lord John Russell had nothing to do but to announce to the Queen that he found it impossible to form a Ministry. The Queen sent for Sir Robert Peel again and asked him to withdraw his resignation. Peel complied, and almost immediately resumed the functions of First Minister of the Crown. The Duke of Buccleuch consented to go on with him, but Lord Stanley held to his resolution and had no place in the Ministry. His position as Secretary of State for the Colonies was taken by Mr. Gladstone. Mr. Gladstone, however, did not sit in Parliament during the eventful session when the corn laws were repealed. He had sat for the borough of Newark, which was under the influence of the Duke of Newcastle, and as the Duke of Newcastle had withdrawn his support from the Ministry, Mr. Gladstone did not seek re-election for Newark, and remained without a seat in the House of Commons for some months.

Parliament met on January 22, 1846. The Speech from the Throne, delivered by the Queen in person, recommended the Legislature to take into consideration the necessity of still further applying the principle on

which it had formerly acted, when measures were presented " to extend commerce and to stimulate domestic
skill and industry, by the repeal of prohibitive and the
relaxation of protective duties." In the debate on the
Address Sir Robert Peel rose, after the mover and sec-
onder had spoken and the question had been put from
the Chair, and at once proceeded to explain the policy
which he intended to.adopt. His speech was long and
laboured, and somewhat wearied the audience by the
elaborate manner in which he explained how his opinions had been brought into gradual change with regard
to Free Trade and Protection. He made it, however,
perfectly clear that he was now a convert to Mr. Cobden's opinions, and that he intended to introduce some
measure which should practically amount to the abolition of Protection. It was in this debate, and immediately after Peel had spoken, that Mr. Disraeli made his
first great impression on Parliament. He had been in
the House for many years and had made many attempts,
had sometimes been laughed at, had sometimes been
disliked, and occasionally for a moment admired. But
it was when he rose immediately after Sir Robert Peel,
and denounced Peel as one who had betrayed his party
and his principles, that he made the first deep impression
on the House of Commons, and came to be considered
as a serious and influential Parliamentary personage.
" I am not one of the converts," Mr. Disraeli said, " I
am perhaps a member of a fallen party." A new Protection party was formed almost immediately under the
leadership of Lord George Bentinck, a man of great
energy and tenacity of purpose, who had hitherto spent
his life almost altogether on the turf, who had had almost
no previous preparation for leadership, or even for debate, but who certainly, when he did accept the respon-

sible position offered to him, showed a considerable capacity for leadership and an unwearying attention to his duties.

On January 27, Sir Robert Peel explained his financial policy. His intention was to abandon the sliding scale altogether, to impose for the present a duty of ten shillings a quarter on corn when the price of it was under forty-eight shillings a quarter, to reduce that duty by one shilling for every shilling of rise in price until it reached fifty-three shillings a quarter, when the duty should fall to four shillings. This, however, was to be only a temporary arrangement. It was to last but three years, and at the end of that time protective duties on grain were to be wholly abandoned. We need not go at any length into the history of the long debates on Peel's propositions. The discussion of one amendment, which was in substance a motion to reject the scheme altogether, lasted for twelve nights. The third reading of the Bill passed the House of Commons on May 15, by a majority of ninety-eight. The Bill went up at once to the House of Lords, and at the urgent pressure of the Duke of Wellington was carried through that House without any serious opposition. The Duke made no secret of his own opinions. He assured many of his brother peers that he disliked the measure just as much as any one could do, but he insisted that they had all better vote for it nevertheless. Sir Robert Peel had triumphed, but he found himself deserted by a large and influential section of the party he once had led. Most of the great landowners and country gentlemen of the Conservative party abandoned him. Some of them felt the bitterest resentment towards him. They believed he had betrayed them, although nothing could be more clear than that for years he had distinctly been making it known to the

House that his principles inclined him towards Free Trade, and thereby leaving it to be understood that, if opportunity or emergency should compel him, he would be glad to declare himself a Free Trader, even in the matter of grain.

Strange to say, the day when the Bill was read in the House of Lords for the third time saw the fall of Peel's Ministry. The fall was due to the state of Ireland. The Government had been bringing in a Coercion Bill for Ireland. It was introduced while the Corn Bill was yet passing through the House of Commons. The situation was critical. All the Irish followers of Mr. O'Connell would be sure to oppose the Coercion Bill. The Liberal party, at least when out of office, had usually made it their principle to oppose Coercion Bills if they were not attended with some promises of legislative reform. The English Radical members, led by Mr. Cobden and Mr. Bright, were certain to oppose coercion. If the Protectionists should join with these other opponents of the Coercion Bill the fate of the measure was assured, and with it the fate of the Government. This was exactly what happened. Eighty Protectionists followed Lord George Bentinck into the lobby against the Bill, in combination with the Free Traders, the Whigs, and the Irish Catholic and national members. The division took place on the second reading of the Bill on Thursday, June 25, and there was a majority of seventy-three against the Ministry. The moment after Sir Robert Peel succeeded in passing his great measure of Free Trade he himself fell from power. His political epitaph, perhaps, could not be better written than in the words with which he closed the speech that just preceded his fall: "It may be that I shall leave a name sometimes remembered with expressions of goodwill in those places which are the abode of men whose lot it is to labour and to earn their daily bread by the sweat of their brow—a name remembered with expressions of goodwill when they shall recreate their exhausted strength with abundant and untaxed food, the sweeter because it is no longer leavened with a sense of injustice."

With the fall of the principle of the protection in corn may be said to have practically fallen the principle of Protection in this country altogether. That principle was a little complicated in regard to the sugar duties and to the navigation laws. The sugar produced in the West Indian colonies was allowed to enter this country at rates of duty much lower than those imposed upon the sugar grown in foreign lands. The abolition of slavery in our colonies had made labour there somewhat costly and difficult to obtain continuously, and the impression was that if the duties on foreign sugar were reduced, it would tend to enable those countries which still maintained the slave trade to compete at great advantage with the sugar grown in our colonies by that free labour to establish which England had but just paid so large a pecuniary fine. Therefore the question of Free Trade became involved with that of free labour; at least, so it seemed to the eyes of many a man who was not inclined to support the protective principle in itself. When it was put to him, whether he was willing to push the Free Trade principle so far as to allow countries growing sugar by slave labour to drive our free grown sugar out of the market, he was often inclined to give way before this mode of putting the question, and to imagine that there really was a collision between Free Trade and free labour. Therefore a certain sentimental plea came in to aid the Protectionists in regard to the sugar duties. Many of the old anti-slavery party found themselves deceived by this fallacy, and inclined to join the agitation against the reduction of the duty on foreign sugar. On the other hand, it was made tolerably clear that the labour was not so scarce or so dear in the colonies as had been represented, and that colonial sugar grown by free labour really suffered from no inconvenience except the fact that it was still manufactured on the most crude, old fashioned, and uneconomical methods. Besides, the time had gone by when the majority of the English people could be convinced that a lesson on the beauty of freedom was to be conveyed to foreign sugar-growers and slave-owners by the means of a tax upon the products of their plantations. Therefore after a long and somewhat eager struggle, the principle of Free Trade was allowed to prevail in regard to sugar. The duties on sugar were made equal. The growth of the sugar plantations was admitted on the same terms into this country, without any reference either to the soil from which it had sprung or to the conditions under which it was grown. It had for a long time been stoutly proclaimed that the abolition of slavery must be the destruction of our West Indian colonies. Years had elapsed and the West Indian colonies still survived. Now the cry of alarm was taken up again, and it was prophesied that although they had got over the abolition of slavery they never could survive the equalisation of the sugar duties. Jamaica certainly had fallen greatly away from her period of temporary and factitious prosperity. Jamaica was owned and managed by a class of proprietors who resembled in many ways some of the planters of the States of America farthest south—of the States towards the mouth of the Mississippi. They lived in a kind of careless luxury, mortgaging their estates as deeply as they possibly could, throwing over to the coming year the superabundant debts of the last, and only managing to keep their heads above water so long as the people of England, by favouring them with a highly protective system, enabled them still to compete against those who grew sugar on better principles and more economical plans. The whole island was given over to neglect and mismanagement. The emancipated negroes took but little trouble to cultivate the plots of ground they had obtained, and were quite content if they could scratch enough from the soil to enable them barely to live. Therefore Jamaica did at a certain time fall far below the level of her former seeming prosperity, The other islands had been better managed. Their estates were less encumbered by debt, and they passed through each successive crisis without sustaining any noticeable injury. In most of these islands the product increased steadily after the emancipation of the slaves. The negroes then began to work earnestly, and education grew not greatly but distinctly amongst all classes. Jamaica, the most unfortunate among the islands, has been constantly the scene of little outbursts of more or less serious rebellion. As the late Lord Chief Justice of England observed in a charge on a famous occasion, "The soil of the island might seem to have been drenched in blood." But these disturbances,. or insurrections, or whatever they may be called, did not increase in number after the abolition of slavery and after the equalisation of the sugar duties, but, on the contrary, decreased. During our time only one considerable disturbance has taken place in Jamaica, and in former years such tumult was of frequent recurrence. In the West Indies we have, therefore, the most severe test to which the principle of Free Trade could well be subjected. It is not too much to say that in the more fortunate of these islands it has established its claim, and that even in the least fortunate no evidence whatever has been given that the people would have been in any way the better off if the old system had been retained.

The navigation laws had, too, a certain external attraction about them which induced many men, not actually Protectionists, to believe in their necessity. The principle of the navigation laws was to impose such restrictions of tariff and otherwise as to exclude foreign vessels from taking any considerable part in our carrying trade. The law was first enacted in Oliver Cromwell's day, at a time when the Dutch were our rivals on the waters, and when it was thought desirable to repress, by protective legislation, the energy of such experienced seamen and pushing traders. The navigation law was modified by Mr. Huskisson in 1823, but only so far as to establish that which we now know so well as the principle of reciprocity. Any nation which removed restrictions from our merchant marine was favoured by us with a similar concession. The idea also was, that these navigation laws, keeping foreigners out of our carrying trade, enabled us to maintain always a supply of sailors who could at any time be transferred from the merchant marine to the Royal Navy, and thus be made to bear their part in the defence of the country. Of course the shipowners themselves upheld the navigation laws, on the plea that, if the trade were thrown open by the withdrawal of Protection, their chances would be gone; that they could not contend against the foreigners upon equal terms; that their interests must suffer, and that Great Britain would in the end be a still severer sufferer, because, from the lack of encouragement given to the native traders and the sailors, England would one day or another be left at the mercy of some strong power which, with wiser regulations, would keep up her protective system and with it her naval strength. Nevertheless, the shipowners, and the Protectionists, and those who raised the alarm cry about England's naval defences, were unable to maintain their sophisms in the face of growing education, and of the impulse given by the adoption of Free Trade. In 1849 the navigation laws were abolished. We believe there are very few shipowners who will not now admit that the prosperity of their trade has grown immensely, in place of suffering from the introduction of the free trade principle in navigation as well as in corn and sugar.

. CHAPTER XIII.

REFORM WITHSTANDS REVOLUTION.

WHILE all these reforms were going on, England was not without revolutionary throbbings. The movement which we call Chartism was, for a while, one that seemed likely to be dangerous. It began at a great Radical meeting held at Birmingham a few weeks after the coronation of Queen Victoria. It sprang into existence chiefly in consequence of a formal declaration made by the leaders of the Liberal party in Parliament, that they did not propose to push reform any further. We have already shown how the Reform Bill passed by Lord Grey and Lord John Russell left the working classes almost entirely out of the franchise. It took away the electoral monopoly from the aristocracy, and transferred it to a combination of aristocracy and plutocracy. It not only did not confer political emancipation on the working classes, but in many places it abolished the peculiar franchise which enabled the working man to be a voter. In some places, such, for example, as the town of Preston, in Lancashire, there was a system of fancy franchise which almost amounted to universal suffrage. The Reform Bill effaced all these peculiarities of suffrage, admitted the middle classes, and the middle classes only, to a share of the law-making power, and shut out the working men altogether. This was the more exasperating to the working classes, because the Reform Bill had been carried in the face of so much resistance, mainly by virtue of their support and their strength. Almost immediately after the opening of the first Parliament of Queen Victoria's reign, a Radical member of the House of Commons moved, as an amendment to the Address, a resolution in favour of the Ballot and of a shorter duration of Parliaments. No more than twenty members supported this amendment, although it contained only the recommendations which men like Lord Durham a few years before were accustomed to propose. During the discussion which took place, Lord John Russell declared distinctly against all attempts to re-open the reform question. The disappointment felt throughout the country, and especially amongst the working classes, was very great. They had been in hopes that the Reform Bill, which they helped to pass, was to be the means by which much greater changes more directly affecting their condition were to be introduced into the Parliamentary system. To their surprise they now heard one of the great leaders of reform declaring that to push the movement any further would be a breach of faith towards those who helped to carry Lord Grey's Bill. Lord John Russell was doubtless right enough in thinking the moment highly inopportune for pushing the reform principle any further. Forward movements in political reform are always, in a country like this, followed by a season of reaction. The House

of Commons was already beginning to feel the influence
of this operation. But, at the same time, it was hard
that working men, who had helped so stoutly to make
the reform movement a success, should be told bluntly
that its influence was to stop short of the only measures
which could in any way affect their condition. A few
Liberal members of Parliament, who professed strong
Radical opinions, held a conference shortly afterwards
with some of the leaders of the working men, and it
appears that at this conference the document which was
afterwards known as the People's Charter was drawn up
and agreed to. O'Connell, it is said, gave it its name.
" There is your Charter," he said to the Secretary of
the Working Men's Association; "agitate for that, and
never be content with anything else."

The Charter was not, after all, a very formidable
document. It insisted on six "points," as they were
called. Manhood suffrage, or as it was then called,
universal suffrage (but its promoters never thought of
the franchise for women), annual Parliaments, vote by
ballot, abolition of the property qualification for the election of a Member of Parliament, payment of Members,
and the division of the country into equal electoral
districts, were the "points" of the famous Charter.
Around the agitation thus got up, there gathered all the
discontented amongst all classes of working men. Some
men of great ability and great earnestness, some men of
more ability than earnestness, took the leadership of the
movement. It had its orators, its poets, its prophets, its
martyrs. Misery and discontent were, however, its
strongest inspiration. The Anti-Corn Law rhymes of
Ebenezer Elliott will show how what he calls the Bread
Tax became identified, and justly, in the minds of working men, with the whole system of political and economi-

cal legislation which was kept up for the benefit of a few. For them the blessings of the British Constitution seemed to mean only incessant exhausting work, miserable wages, and scanty food. The Government endeavoured to repress Chartist meetings and Chartist disturbances by force. They prosecuted some of the spokesmen and leaders of the Chartist movement, and Henry Vincent, a man of good character and a certain amount of eloquence, was imprisoned at Newport in Wales. His imprisonment was the cause of the famous attempt of Frost, Williams, and Jones, which, beginning with a scheme merely for the release of Vincent from jail, grew into a sort of insurrection. A conflict took place between the Chartists and the soldiery and the police, in which the Chartists were dispersed with a loss of eight or ten men and fifty or sixty wounded. Frost and his companions were tried on a charge of high treason, were found guilty, and sentenced to death, but the sentence was commuted to one of transportation for life. Their conviction did not put a stop to the Chartist agitation. On the contrary, Chartism seemed to have received a new life and a new direction since the failure of the attempt at Newport. A new race of Chartists began to spring up. The convictions of Frost and his companions stirred up sympathy amongst men who, up to that time, had not even had their attention turned to the movement.

About the same time that the Chartist disturbances were going on in this country the repeal agitation was spreading over Ireland. The repeal movement was started by Daniel O'Connell, with the object of dissolving the tie which bound two countries into one system of Government. O'Connell was a man of extraordinary eloquence, energy, and ability. He was as shrewd in council as he was commanding in speech. He has hardly ever had a rival as a popular orator. The universal opinion of his time pronounced him to be the greatest platform speaker of that day, and although he entered the House of Commons late in life, when he was almost midway between fifty and sixty, he yet achieved a reputation in that highly-cultured assembly scarcely inferior, if inferior at all, to the fame he had won out of doors. It was mainly through his energy and determination that Catholic emancipation was at last forced upon a reluctant Ministry. After Catholic emancipation he was disappointed with the course the Whigs were taking, and he set himself to organize an agitation for the repeal of the legislative union between England and Ireland. The Act of Union, whatever its objects might have been, was undoubtedly brought about by measures and means over which, to use Carlyle's words, "moralities not a few must shriek aloud." The most audacious and wholesale system of bribery had been employed to accomplish the Union. Peers were made and votes were bought as rapidly and as openly as if there was no need even for pretending to disguise the purpose of these transactions. Lord Cornwallis, who conducted the negotiations at the time in Ireland, again and again expressed to his friends his disgust and loathing for the work he had to do. It is therefore easy to understand that O'Connell found strong feeling enough against the Union already in the minds of his countrymen to admit of his easily rousing them up into a fury against it. He organized a great system of monster meetings. He may be regarded as the author and inventor of that practice of modern agitation which has now taken possession of the whole English-speaking world. He gave something of a military appearance to the crowds who attended his meetings. They marched in martial array with bands and banners. It is not likely

that O'Connell ever intended anything like an armed rebellion ; but it is probable that he was anxious to make
the Government believe that he had the force at his back
whenever he chose to call it into action. He had an
entire command of the peasantry, of the priests, and of the
artisans in the towns, and of most of the Catholic traders
and shopkeepers of whatever class in the towns also.
Nobody in Ireland, before his time, had anything like the
same command of the whole national public opinion of
the country. Had he but held up his hand at any
moment he could have made a rebellion. This, however, was not O'Connell's policy. He hoped, by a frequent display of popular strength, to force the Government into the concession of the claim which he made.
It would not have suited his purpose either to begin a
rebellion or to have it distinctly known that he never intended to begin one. The Government, at last taking
alarm at his menacing demonstrations, prohibited one of
his monster meetings. O'Connell acted with great
promptitude. He instantly issued a proclamation of his
own advising the people to disperse in quiet. Always
obedient to his command the immense crowds which had
been pouring into the place of meeting broke up quietly
and went to their homes again. But the course taken
by O'Connell was fatal to his popularity. With the
young men especially it wore away his influence. Most
of them fully believed that he intended an armed
struggle at some time or another, and when they found
now, by his own positive assurance and by his own
action, that he had no such purpose their interest in the
movement faded away. His judgment, of course, was
much shrewder and better than theirs, but their youth-
ful enthusiasm could not abide disappointment. O'Connell was afterwards prosecuted for seditious speaking,

tried, found guilty, and sentenced to fine and imprisonment.   He appealed to the House of Lords against the
sentence, on the ground that jury lists had been prepared
in such a manner as to insure his conviction.   A majority
of the House of Lords affirmed that the judgment ought
not to be sustained.   The occasion was remarkable
because, among other reasons, it marked a new chapter
in the practice of the House of Lords.   The constitution
of the House of Lords recognised at that time, and for a
long time afterwards, no difference between the law lords
and the other peers in voting on any question of appeal.
The lay peers indeed hardly ever exercised their right
to vote.   But they had the right to do so and there were
some cases in which they had put it into practice and
voted on appeal just as if they had been masters of the
law.   If the lay lords had exercised their right in the
case of O'Connell, it is certain that the decision ·of the
court below would have been maintained.   No one had
ever denounced the House of Lords with more bitterness
and virulence than O'Connell.   On the other hand, it is
certain that the sincere opinion of a majority of the
House of Lords was that O'Connell well deserved his
condemnation and his sentence.   The moment was
critical.   Nothing could possibly have had a more evil
effect on public opinion in Ireland than the decision of a
question purely of law by the votes of peers who were
not lawyers, and against a man who had made himself
their most conspicuous personal enemy.   Lord Wharncliffe suddenly arose and appealed to the wiser judgment
and calmer temper of his brother peers.   He begged of
them not to take a course which might leave it open to
O'Connell and to everyone to say that political and
personal feeling had governed a judicial decision of the
House of Lords.   Just before Lord Wharncliffe spoke

one lay peer at least had declared that he would insist upon his right to vote. Several others gave it to be understood that they were determined to follow the example. Lord Wharncliffe's timely interposition had a happy effect. All the lay peers tacitly acknowledged the justice of his advice. They withdrew from the House and left the decision, according to the usual fashion, in the hands of the law lords. The majority of these, as we have said, were against the judgment of the court below, and O'Connell and his companions were set at liberty. The lay peers never again voted on a question of judicial appeal, so long as the appellate jurisdiction of the House of Lords was still allowed to remain in their hands after the traditional and anomalous fashion.

The appeal agitation faded. It gave way, however, only to a more impassioned and more energetic association. This was the Young Ireland confederation. A number of eager and passionate young men, weary and impatient of O'Connell's policy, broke away from him shortly before his death, and founded an association of their own. It gradually and rapidly glided into something like rebellion. It would probably have gone that way in any case, because there could be no succession to O'Connell's movement which would not be an anticlimax unless it assumed the open form of rebellion. But the Young Ireland movement, like the Chartist movement in England, was inflamed with new life and passion and fire by the outbreak of the French Revolution of 1848.

The year 1848 was a year of revolution. The flame which broke out in France spread over the whole Continent. From Madrid to Moscow, from Paris to Constantinople, the movement was felt. Thrones were coming down in all directions. Whole systems were crashing like old houses in some ancient quarters of a city in a night of storm. The revolutionary impulse began in France, but of the fatuity with which Louis Philippe and his Minister were striving to carry restriction and repression too far. The fall of Guizot and of Louis Philippe with him was distinctly owing to the cause to which Sir Robert Peel ascribed it. Peel heard in the House of Commons from Mr. Joseph Hume the news of the fate of the French Monarchy, and quietly remarked that that was what came of trying to govern a country on too narrow a basis of representation. M. Guizot, a man of great ability and sound judgment as an historian, was singularly perverse and narrow when he came to deal with actual systems and living men. It was his conviction that he could manage to govern France by means of a restricted principle of representation, so that the country should have all the appearance of a representative system while in reality it was ruled by the Minister and the Court. He pushed his doctrine too far, and the result was a popular uprising, which complete concession might have satisfied in time, but which, complete concession being denied, broke out before long into revolution. Louis Philippe fled from Paris and became an exile in England. It was said and believed for a long time that he owed his fall from the throne to his reluctance to use forcible measures for the repression of the popular rising. Recent publications, however, and recent accounts of conversations with M. Thiers, show that there is no truth in the report which ascribed to the late King of the French such a chivalrous or quixotic sentiment of humanity. He would have suppressed the revolution by any exertion of military force and at any cost of human life if he had only seen his way in time.

After the proclamation of the Republic in France, the revolutionary spirit flew over the whole of Europe. It broke out in Prussia, in Austria, in Italy—almost everywhere. The popular rising in Austria proved so powerful that for a time it was thought there was little hope of the then reigning Emperor being able to maintain his place in Vienna. Venice proclaimed herself a Republic, and under the leadership of the noble and pure-hearted Daniel Manin, held her own for no inconsiderable time. Charles Albert, the King of Sardinia, was compelled to put himself at the head of the popular movement in Italy, although he had himself at one time used stern measures for the repression of a popular uprising. The Austrians were for a while virtually dispossessed of the Lombard provinces. Pope Pius IX., who had at first shown a strong inclination to become the leader of the national movement against the Austrians and foreigners of all kinds, suddenly drew back before the danger of bloodshed and the difficulty of dealing with a great revolutionary crisis, and the immediate result was that revolution broke out in Rome itself. The Pope had to take refuge in Gaeta, in the dominions of the King of Naples, and a Republic was proclaimed in Rome under a triumvirate, with Joseph Mazzini at its head. A rising took place in Berlin, and the streets of the city were drenched in blood. A revolt broke out in Baden, and was suppressed not without some difficulty by the troops of the King of Prussia. Hungry, which had long been murmuring against the restriction of her ancient liberties and the abolition of her time-honored constitution by Austria, rose in a gigantic rebellion against the house of Hapsburg. On many great battle-fields the Hungarians met the Austrians, and were the victors; and it may be almost taken for granted that Hungary would have asserted successfully her entire independence of Austria at that time, but that Nicholas, the Emperor of Russia, seeing his own frontiers threatened by the rush of the revolutionary movement, intervened on behalf of Austria, and by means of his enormous forces succeeded in defeating the Hungarians in the field, and in finally compelling their submission. Their dictator, Kossuth, took refuge at first in Turkey, and afterwards came to England. The King of the Belgians escaped the storm of revolution by the courage with which he confronted it. In the words of Hamlet, he may be said to have " taken arms against a sea of troubles," but not arms in the military sense. He encountered the difficulty by announcing from his palace windows that he had escaped the Crown of Belgium as the free gift of the Belgian people, and that he was ready at any moment to put it down and to leave the country if the Belgian people no longer wished him to retain his place. The result was what might have been expected from an attitude so chivalrous and kingly. The Belgians insisted on his retaining the Crown ; and he continued to be, to his death, one of the most popular sovereigns in Europe.

The movement on the Continent proved to be premature. It was repressed in every single instance, with the exception of France alone, and even there the repression was but put off for a year or two. The movement in Northern Italy was after a while completely crushed out. Charles Albert was defeated hopelessly and finally at Novara, and he shortly afterwards thought it wise to abdicate his throne in favor of his son Victor Emmanuel, and retired to exile in Portugal, where he died. We have described the fate of the Hungarian movement. The French Government sent troops to Rome, and afterwards intervened against the Revolution

and for the restoration of Pope Pius. Venice was re-
captured by the Austrians, and Manin became an exile.
For no inconsiderable time it seemed as if reaction had
obtained complete control of the continental peoples,
and as if the day of constitutional freedom was indefi-
nitely postponed.

Meanwhile, how did England fare ? England's history
during all that crisis is a striking illustration of the
manner in which the principle of reform acts as a rampart
against revolution. The flame of continental revolt
spread itself to this country and to Ireland. In England
the Chartist movement sprang up into fierce, and what
seemed at one time very dangerous activity. In Ireland,
the young men, clever, brilliant, sincere, young men for
the most part, who had seceded from the leadership of
O Connell, began open preparations for an armed rebellion. The Chartist movement burst like a bubble, on
Kennington Common, on April 10, 1848. The Young
Ireland party were hurried into a premature outbreak in
the summer of the same year, and it was suppressed
almost before the Irish population in general knew that
it had begun. Neither in England nor in Ireland did
the disturbance call for a single charge of cavalry. The
explanation of all this is clear. It is not that there were
no grievances in England and Ireland to justify the
strongest protest. There were still grievances that
would have been intolerable if men could have supposed
that they were likely to last. There were grievances
which would well have warranted a revolutionary uprising against them, if it could have been supposed that
there was no other way of getting rid of them. But all
reasonable men knew that they could be got rid of; that
only time and patience and the working of public opinion
were needed for their removal. The reforms already

accomplished were guarantee of further reforms, and the people knew that they could afford to wait.

The reform movement, which was conducted to practical statesmanship by Lord Grey and Lord John Russell, went on, making its influence felt in all directions. Religious equality, commercial freedom, popular education, the opening of universities to all sects, the extension of the suffrage—these are some of the operations of the principle which was put into force when the Reform Bill of 1832 was passed. There have of course been intervals of reaction, but the progress of reform has been steady on the whole. Since 1848 we have never heard even a whisper of domestic disturbance in England. Every reasonable man knows that the work of pacification in Ireland is only a question of just and generous legislation.

Perhaps we cannot bring our account of this epoch of reform more fittingly to a close than with the death of Sir Robert Peel. On the morning of June 29, 1850, Sir Robert Peel left the House of Commons shortly before four o'clock. He went home for rest, but it could only be rest for a brief interval. He had to go to a meeting of the commissioners of the Great Exhibition at twelve. He went to the meeting and bore a part in the discussion. He returned home for a short time and then went out for a ride in the park. As he was riding up Constitution Hill, he stopped to talk to a lady, the daughter of a friend. His horse suddenly started and flung him off. Peel clung to the bridle. The horse fell with its knees on his shoulders. He received such injuries as to render his recovery impossible. He lingered for two or three days, sometimes conscious, sometimes unconscious, and he died toward midnight on July 2. His death closed appropriately a great period of reform. Peel was a reformer forced into reform. He had not accepted it of his own impulse. We find him through the greater part of his career resisting every proposal for change in the beginning, and yet becoming himself identified with some of the greatest changes in the political history of the time. Lord Beaconsfield speaks of him as a great member of Parliament, and uses the phrase in a manner which seems to imply that in Lord Beaconsfield's opinion he was that and that alone. But Sir Robert Peel was undoubtedly a great minister of state and even a great statesman as well. He was a profoundly conscientious man. His reason and conscience were alike active and alike exercised command over him. He was one of the small number of statesmen who are willing to renounce their dearest opinions, the traditions of their youth, the prejudices of their manhood, if their reason can only be convinced that other opinions are just. Sir Robert Peel's great change on the question of the corn laws does as much credit to his intellect as to his conscience. He could not close his mind against the arguments of the free traders, and his conscience would not allow him to shape his political course in any other way but as his reason directed. Sir Robert Peel was not indeed a man of original genius. His greatest triumphs were accomplished by the adaptation of other men's ideas. No two men, perhaps, could seem to be less alike than Peel and Mirabeau, and yet Peel and Mirabeau resembled each other in this, that each had a marvellous power of assimilating the ideas of others and putting them into action in practical politics. Peel was a great administrator and a great Parliamentary debater, and he had so thorough an understanding of all the principles of finance that he first and last won for the conservative party the repute of being the sound economists and trustworthy financiers of the country. Before his time and after his time, Whig or Liberal Governments have always claimed, and been allowed, the credit of financial skill and success. Sir Robert Peel, in his prime, carried the sceptre of finance fairly over to the Conservative ranks, and kept it there until his death. He was a man of austere character and somewhat chilly temperament, awkward and shy in manner. People thought him proud where he was only reserved. He was really full of warmth and generous feeling, but his sensitive character led him to disguise his emotions, and this contrast between his strong feelings and his want of demonstrativeness, gave him a certain artificial manner which seemed merely awkward. His real genius and character came out in the House of Commons and in debate. He was not an orator of the highest class. He had little passion and almost no imagination, but his style was clear, strong, and flowing. His speeches are full of various argument and appropriate illustration. They were the very perfection of good sense and high principle, clothed in the most impressive language. At the time of his death Peel was still in the fullest possession of all his faculties, both of mind and body. He was little more than sixty-two years of age, and it seemed almost certain that he had a great career still before him. He would probably have become Prime Minister again, or else he would have filled a post still more important than that occupied for many years by the Duke of Wellington, that of impartial adviser to the Sovereign, no matter what party happened to be in power, trusted alike by the Sovereign, by parties, and by the people. He would have filled this place better than the Duke of Wellington did, for although no man could be more simply sincere than was the Duke in his patriotic desire to serve his Sovereign, Peel had a mind so far

superior in flexibility and in strength, that he would have
known, what the Duke of Wellington did not always
know, how to reconcile devotion to the Sovereign with
loyalty to the people, and the recognition of new ideas
and new political conditions. If we are not to class Peel
amongst great ministers of the first rank, it is, perhaps,
only because, during his time, England was not put to
any trial of the kind that calls out the greatest faculties
of statesmanship, and wins for men a name with the
foremost in history.

CHAPTER XIV.

A SURVEY, POLITICAL AND SOCIAL.

ENGLAND'S imperial responsibilities grow greater year
by year with the continued increase of her colonial possessions. She has, however, wisely provided against the
difficulty of governing far distant colonies from a central
point in Westminster, by gradually allowing to each of
her great colonies a system of self-government. Not
long after the accession of Queen Victoria, Lord Durham,
sent out as commissioner to endeavour to reorganise
the affairs of Canada after a rebellion there, succeeded
in laying the foundations of a system of self-government,
which has gradually been expanding until it has taken in
nearly all the British possessions in North America under
one federation. The colonies in Australasia have also
been gradually brought up to this system of self-government. New South Wales, the oldest of the group, came
into constitutional and political life about the time at
which this history closes. Victoria was separated from
New South Wales in 1851, and brought her constitutional
system into working order a few years after. The other
colonies followed by degrees. The discovery of gold in

Australia was an event of immense importance both to the colony and to England. It sent a sudden rush of emigration from all countries out to Victoria, and the result was, that in a very few years the great and flourishing city of Melbourne, grew up on a shore that had previously been only a landing place for men pushing their way inland to cultivate farms and raise cattle and sheep. Gold was discovered in Australia in 1851, and had been discovered in California three or four years before. Since then gold has been found in many other of our colonies, and always with the same result of directing a sudden emigration to the place, and leading to the birth of great communities and the building of large towns. Independently, however, of the discovery of gold emigration to the colonies had greatly developed during the years which we have surveyed. The English language thus spreads all over the world, and promises before long to be the tongue most common amongst civilized nations. To the great Indian Empire enough of attention had not been paid for many years by statesmen and the public at home. Our public men here knew but little of the struggle of races and conflict of interests which were going on in India. Territories were annexed, rulers were deposed, and successions were cut off rather heedlessly from time to time, by Indian viceroys obeying perhaps the spur of immediate expediency rather than keeping their eyes fixed upon the responsibilities of the future. The English people were therefore taken wholly by surprise when the great Indian Mutiny broke out, a few years after the period at which we have now arrived, and brought about, as one result, the reorganisation of the system of government in India and the abolition of the old East India Company.

About the time of Peel's death the Eastern Question

began to occupy the attention of Europe. What is the
Eastern Question? It is, in plain words, the question,
What is to become of the dominions now occupied by the
Turkish Government in Europe and in Asia. The Turks
settled themselves in Europe in the fifteenth century.
They captured Constantinople, overran a great part of
the south-west of the Continent, and pushed their invasion so far as to threaten Vienna, the Capital of Austria.
They obtained what seemed for a long time a secure
holding of all, or nearly all, the dominions of the later
Roman Empire, that is to say, all the Empire which had
its capital in Constantinople. They brought into Europe
a political and social system entirely out of harmony
with western civilisation. While the Turks were strong,
all the powers of Europe were banded together against
them, and would have joined eagerly in any movement
which seemed likely to drive the Ottoman back into
Asia. But when, of later years, Turkey began to grow
weak, when her internal affairs became disorganised,
when province after province began to show itself impatient of her rule, then a new condition arose, which
not only prevented some of the Western Powers from
desiring to see the Turks driven out of Europe, but even
induced them to unite for the purpose of maintaining
them in their possessions. This new condition was the
growth of the Russian Empire. Russia was becoming
powerful as the Turks began to grow weak. She was
eager to extend her dominions to the south. The dread
which many modern statesmen felt, was that Russia
would make herself mistress of all the provinces now
held by the Turks in Europe, and thus become a far
greater danger to other European Powers than the
Turkish Empire in its crippled modern condition could
possibly be. Therefore a school of statesmen sprang

into existence, who maintained that it was part of the national duty and interest of England to maintain that Empire, and another school came up almost equally strong, whose doctrine was that the power of the Sultan must inevitably crumble to pieces, and that we ought to make every preparation for its decay, by encouraging the European provinces to form themselves into separate and independent states. English interests, too, were further concerned in the condition of the Turks because of the relationship which Egypt holds at once to the Sultan and to England. It is of the utmost importance for England that no foreign power should get possession of Egypt, because Egypt is a necessary part of our high road to India. So long as the Sultan holds Egypt, and the Sultan himself is to a certain extent under the protection of England, we are sure Egypt is safe. The school of statesmen who hold that it is essential for our interests to maintain the Ottoman Empire, make it a part of their argument, that if we do not maintain it, we should have to occupy Egypt ourselves, or to submit to its being occupied by some foreign power, which might perhaps some day stand between us and our way to India.

The year 1850 did not seem one of good augury for the progress of free political institutions on the European continent. The spirit of the national party of Hungary appeared to be crushed. Foreign occupation and intervention were once more triumphant over the greater part of Italy. The hopes which German populations had been forming of a United Germany, under the leadership of Prussia, appeared to be blighted. Prussia had fallen to be a mere dependent or creature now of Austria and now of Russia. The manner in which Prussian politics were made subservient to the intrigues of Russia filled the heart of many a patriotic German with anger and despair, and contributed not a little to the causes and influences which afterwards brought about the Crimean War. In the domestic Government of almost all the continental States an iron despotism, a rigid police system reigned supreme. In France the sudden establishment of the Republic, with its weaknesses and errors, had only served to open a way for Louis Napoleon, nephew of the great Napoleon, and for a long time an exile in England, to get himself elected President; and from the chair of the President he made his way before long to an Imperial throne. In August 1850, Louis Philippe, formerly King of the French, died at his residence in England. A few days later the President Louis Napoleon, at a banquet in Cherbourg, in France, was hailed with cries of "Long live the Emperor." A month later Louis Napoleon was reviewing the troops on the plain of Satory, near Paris. As some of the cavalry regiments passed by, they shouted first "Long live the President," and afterwards "Long live the Emperor." Already men began to look forward with something like certainty to the change which was about to take place in the Government of France, and which only a little later was accomplished by the memorable *coup d'état* of December 2, 1851.

The wave of popular revolution seemed to have wholly subsided. Autocratic rule appeared to have a new charter of life conferred upon it. Not since the meeting of the Allied Sovereigns at Verona, and the publishing of the Holy Alliance, had arbitrary authority seemed so securely established all over continental Europe. Yet we have only to look forward a little way ·in order to see how the very same sort of reaction which followed the Holy Alliance, followed the re-establishment of personal authority in Europe. Before very long

Hungary had quietly secured her independence. The Austrians had to give up Lombardy in 1859 and Venetia in 1866. Italy gradually became united into one kingdom. Prussia made herself the predominant power in Germany. Austria was forced to recede altogether from her place in the German system. The French Empire fell in 1870, and a Republic was established in its place. Meanwhile, nothing could be more remarkable than the contrast between the condition of England and that of the Continent. In England there had been no political uprising of any kind which could call for a serious reaction. The Chartist disturbances and the momentary outbreak of revolution in Ireland had passed away with comparatively little harm done. The progress which political life had been steadily making in these islands, and the certainty that what further reform was yet needed was to be accomplished best by peaceful means and by patience, had had their inevitable effect. While continental Europe was once more broken up by revolt and reaction, England was pursuing steadily the path of peaceful reform. While the Government of Austria were still executing some of their Hungarian rebels, and were chafing and fuming because Kossuth, the Hungarian leader, had escaped from their power; while the President of the French Republic was silently arranging for his *coup d'état*, England, under the inspiration of the late Prince Consort, was busily engaged in preparing for the first Great Exhibition of the Works of All Nations, to be held in the Crystal Palace in Hyde Park.

It was not, however, in political affairs alone that these islands had been making steady progress during all this time. Indeed, it would not be possible for any people to make any advance in political reform without making social and moral progress as well; or perhaps it should rather he said that without the growth of improvement in intelligence and in moral feeling, the improvement in politics could not take place.   It would be impossible for anyone to survey the lengthened period which we have been describing without being struck by the steady advance made in the social condition of England.   We have shown how many great reforms were made in the criminal laws, how the severity of punishments was mitigated, and how the mitigation of the penal code was assisted further by legislation intended to make life less hard upon the poor, and, therefore, to give less temptation to crime.   The factory legislation, the laws for the regulation of mines and collieries—these were improvements thoroughly in the spirit of the age.   Society itself improved.   At the period with which this history begins the duelling system was still a fashionable institution.   Not only military men and hot-tempered youth settled their quarrels with the pistol, but grave statesmen and elderly lawyers had recourse to the same means of finishing a dispute.   The Duke of Wellington fought a duel with Lord Winchilsea ; Sir Robert Peel was making arrangements to fight a duel with O'Connell when the interference of friends brought the dispute to a conclusion ; Mr. Disraeli challenged one of O'Connell's sons because O'Connell himself declined to fight.   It is in great measure to the influence of the late Prince Consort that the decay and final abandonment of the duelling system in this country is to be ascribed.   Some singularly tragic and painful quarrels, futile in their original purpose, had drawn public attention directly to the hideousness of the practice, and the intervention at such a timely moment of the Prince Consort, and the use he made of his influence with the military authorities, had much to do in helping forward the great moral and social reform.   The barbarous amusements which during the reign even of William IV. were still common among all classes, such as bull-baiting and cock-fighting, have now ceased to be the pastime of even the rudest and most ignorant. We do not pretend to say that all this advance has been made without some corresponding reaction, but, taken on the whole, a marked improvement in the moral tone of society, from the highest to the lowest, is distinctly to be noted, and might be proved almost by the test of arithmetical figures. The numerous improvements which have been made in the drainage of cities, in the ventilation of houses, in the providing of gardens and open spaces for the poor children of large towns to play in ; all these beneficent changes could not fail to produce a decided effect upon the general health of the population. The shocking habits of drunkenness which at one time pervaded all classes of men in this country are now confined mainly to the uneducated and to the poor, whose rigorous lot and almost incessant toil makes temptation not easy to resist. It may, moreover, be confidently hoped that in time a vice which has faded away from all the more educated classes of society will leave society altogether, and that the spread of education amongst the very poorest will bring sobriety with it.

The Standard Edition of Gladstone's Essays.

Gleanings of Past Years.

BY

The Right Hon. W. E. GLADSTONE.

Seven Volumes, 16mo, Cloth, per volume, $1.00.

The extraordinary scope of Mr. Gladstone's learning—the wonder of his friends and enemies alike—and his firm grasp of every subject he discusses, make his essays much more than transient literature. Their collection and publication in permanent shape were of course certain to be undertaken sooner or later; and now that they are so published with the benefit of his own revision, they will need little heralding in England or America.

What Mr. Gladstone has written in the last thirty-six years—the period covered by this collection—has probably had the attention of as large an English-speaking public as any writer on political and social topics ever reached in his own life-time. The papers which he has chosen as of lasting value, and included here under the title of *Gleanings of Past Years*, will form the standard edition of his miscellanies, both for his present multitude of readers, and for those who will study his writings later.

Vol. I. The Throne, and the Prince Consort; The Cabinet, and Constitution.

Vol. II.—Personal and Literary.

Vol. III.—Historical and Speculative.

Vol. IV.—Foreign.

Vol. V. ⎱ Ecclesiastical.
Vol. VI. ⎰

Vol. VII.—Miscellaneous.

**The above books for sale by all booksellers, or will be sent, prepaid, upon receipt of price, by

CHARLES SCRIBNER'S SONS, Publishers,

743 AND 745 Broadway, New York.

Perry's Political Economy.

Epochs of Modern History.

Each 1 vol. 16mo., with Outline Maps.   Price per volume, In cloth, $1.00.

EACH VOLUME COMPLETE IN ITSELF AND SOLD SEPARATELY.

EDITED BY EDWARD E. MORRIS, M.A.

The ERA of the PROTESTANT REVOLUTION. By F. SEEBOHM. Author of "The Oxford Reformers—Colet, Erasmus, More."

The CRUSADES. By the Rev. G. W. Cox, M.A., Author of the "History of Greece."

The THIRTY YEARS' WAR, 1618—1648. By SAMUEL RAWSON GARDINER.

The HOUSES of LANCASTER and YORK; with the CONQUEST and LOSS of FRANCE. By JAMES GAIRDNER, of the Public Record Office.

The FRENCH REVOLUTION and FIRST EMPIRE; an Historical Sketch. By WM. O'CONNOR MORRIS, with an Appendix by Hon. ANDREW D. WHITE, Prest. of Cornell University.

The AGE OF ELIZABETH. By the Rev. M. CREIGHTON, M.A.

The PURITAN REVOLUTION. By J. LANGTON SANFORD.

The FALL of the STUARTS; and WESTERN EUROPE from 1678 to 1697. By the Rev. EDWARD HALE, M.A., Assist. Master at Eton.

The EARLY PLANTAGENETS and their relation to the HISTORY of EUROPE ; the foundation and growth of CONSTITUTIONAL GOVERNMENT. By the Rev. WM. STUBBS, M.A., etc., Regius Professor of Modern History in the University of Oxford.

The BEGINNING of the MIDDLE AGES: CHARLES the GREAT and ALFRED ; the HISTORY of ENGLAND in its connection with that of EUROPE in the NINTH CENTURY. By the Very Rev R. W. CHURCH, M.A., Dean of St. Paul's.

The AGE of ANNE. By EDWARD E. MORRIS, M.A., Editor of the Series.

The NORMANS IN EUROPE. By the Rev. A. H. JOHNSON, M. A.

The above Twelve Volumes in Roxburgh Style, Leather Labels and Gilt Top Put up in a handsome Box. Sold only in Sets. Price per Set, $12.00.

FREDERICK the GREAT and the SEVEN YEARS' WAR. By F. W LONGMAN, of Ballic College, Oxford.

₊ *The above book for sale by all booksellers, or will be sent, post or express charges paid, upon receipt of the price by the publishers.*

CHARLES SCRIBNER'S SONS,

743 AND 745 BROADWAY, NEW YORK.

A New Edition, Library Style.

The History of Rome,

FROM THE EARLIEST TIME TO THE PERIOD OF ITS DECLINE.

By Dr. THEODOR MOMMSEN.

Translated, with the author's sanction and additions, by the Rev. W. P. Dickson, Regius Professor of Biblical Criticism in the University of Glasgow, late Classical Examiner of the University of St. Andrews. With an introduction by Dr. Leonhard Schmitz, and a copious Index of the whole four volumes, prepared especially for this edition.

REPRINTED FROM THE REVISED LONDON EDITION.

Four Volumes, crown 8vo, gilt top.   Price per Set, $8.00.

———♦———

Dr. Mommsen has long been known and appreciated through his researches into the languages, laws, and institutions of Ancient Rome and Italy, as the most thoroughly versed scholar now living in these departments of historical investigation. To a wonderfully exact and exhaustive knowledge of these subjects, he unites great powers of generalization, a vigorous, spirited, and exceedingly graphic style and keen analytical powers, which give this history a degree of interest and a permanent value possessed by no other record of the decline and fall of the Roman Commonwealth. "Dr. Mommsen's work," as Dr. Schmitz remarks in the introduction, "though the production of a man of most profound and extensive learning and knowledge of the world, is not as much designed for the professional scholar as for intelligent readers of all classes who take an interest in the history of by-gone ages, and are inclined there to seek information that may guide them safely through the perplexing mazes of modern history."

CRITICAL NOTICES.

" A work of the very highest merit ; its learning is exact and profound ; its narrative full of genius and skill ; its descriptions of men are admirably vivid. We wish to place on record our opinion that Dr. Mommsen's is by far the best history of the Decline and Fall of the Roman Commonwealth." — *London Times.*

"This is the best history of the Roman Republic, taking the work on the whole — the author's complete mastery of his subject, the variety of his gifts and acquirements, his graphic power in the delineation of national and individual character, and the vivid interest which he inspires in every portion of his book. He is without an equal in his own sphere." — *Edinburgh Review.*

CHARLES SCRIBNER'S SONS, Publishers,

743 and 745 Broadway, New York.

Communism and Socialism

IN THEIR HISTORY AND THEORY.

A SKETCH

By THEODORE D. WOOLSEY, D.D., LL.D.

One Volume, 12mo, $1.50.

This book is the only comprehensive review of its subject, within small compass, yet exactly meeting the needs of the reader, that is accessible in English. The candor of the discussion is remarkable; the book is the argument of a perfectly fair reasoner, painting nothing in too dark colors, but taking his opponents at their best. It may be safely prophesied that beyond the large audience which will take up this thoroughly excellent little volume for purposes of study, there will be a still wider one who will read it from pure interest in the history of communities and social experiments, from the Essenes and Therapeutæ down to the International.

CRITICAL NOTICES.

" The calm, thoughtful, and logical view this volume takes of the subject should recommend it to the attention of readers of every degree."— *Boston Saturday Evening Gazette.*

" The work is an epitome of the whole history of the socialistic and communistic movement, and will prove a most valuable text-book to all who have not made themselves familiar with this great subject."—*N. Y. Commercial Advertiser.*

" Altogether, this little book contains a completer view of the complicated forms of socialism than can be elsewhere found within similar compass, and may safely be taken as a guide by students and thinkers of all shades of opinion."—*N. Y. Herald.*

" The discussion of the history and theory of the various forms of communism and socialism contained in this volume is marked by the comprehensive research, clearness of perception, sobriety of judgment, and fairness of statement characteristic of the author. . . . . No previous writer on the subject has exhibited so clear a perception of the vital points at issue, or has offered more sound and wholesome counsels in regard to their treatment."—*N. Y. Tribune.*

** For sale by all booksellers, or sent, post-paid, upon receipt of price, by

CHARLES SCRIBNER'S SONS, Publishers,

743 and 745 Broadway, New York.

www.ingramcontent.com/pod-product-compliance
Lightning Source LLC
Chambersburg PA
CBHW020114030726
47498CB00006B/2099